"A riveting back and forth between compelling principles of contextualized apologetics and life story. Luke speaks powerfully and prophetically about what apologetics in our day should look like as he gives the reader a fresh glimpse of what happens when our head and heart come together in our striving with people. Luke has an obvious love for God and for people. He paints a picture of what it looks like to do an apologetic and evangelistic ministry with impact and compassion. Theory, practice, heart, passion and presence—few books bring this level of integration together as *The Myth of the Non-Christian!*"

R. York Moore, national evangelist, InterVarsity Christian Fellowship/USA

"I have read many books on helping people to faith in Christ, but this is one of the best. Perceptive, well read, full of illustrative stories and extremely practical. Buy it and use it!"

Michael Green, theologian and evangelist

"I've been equipped and inspired anew by this book to better understand and connect with the many different kinds of people who don't yet follow Jesus. Ditch the one-size-fits-all approach to being a witness: let this book help you do the things that may actually meet our friends' felt spiritual needs."

James Choung, national director of evangelism, InterVarsity Christian Fellowship/USA

"Luke Cawley's book is a brilliant resource for anyone interested in any form of Christian apologetics—for evangelists, teachers, pastors and indeed for anyone who wants to engage those who don't understand what Christ offers that the culture cannot. The book is full of captivating snippets of conversations you and I have every day. It will make every reader more able to understand those who do not know Christ and more able to present him in ways they can understand. Cawley covers the gamut of unbelievers—skeptics, atheists, the unchurched and the spiritual but not religious. Importantly, Cawley is not afraid to engage the serious topic of spiritual reality. The text is highly accessible without compromising depth and should be read by all who ever want to talk with nonbelievers."

Mary Poplin, professor and author of *Is Real*

"I am convinced that we need to rethink evangelism in light of the increasingly missionary situation of the church in our time. This is a top-class book that will help God's people do just that. We might just become a more genuinely good-news people in the process."

Alan Hirsch, author and activist

"The world of real estate is ruled by one word repeated thrice: location, location, location. In the real world of relationships, which is the *real* estate of life, one word reigns supreme: context, context, context. Luke Cawley has written the new go-to book for contextual apologetics. This book is everywhere thoughtful and judicious; it is wide-ranging and deeply illuminating."

Leonard Sweet, E. Stanley Jones Professor of Evangelism, Drew University, bestselling author of *From Tablet to Table*, creator of preachthestory.com

"While many people think of apologetics and cringe for fear of engaging in heated, insensitive arguments, *The Myth of the Non-Christian* presents a refreshingly different perspective. Listen to people, love them, help them connect to Jesus in a way that makes sense to them. It's a simple yet profound concept that can transform the ways we engage people with the gospel. Luke Cawley winsomely communicates to people of diverse backgrounds that following Jesus makes intellectual sense and satisfies our deepest longings. This book is a gift to all of us who are seeking to share this message!"

Jessica Leep Fick, author of *Beautiful Feet*

The Myth of the Non-Christian

Engaging Atheists, Nominal Christians
and the Spiritual But Not Religious

Luke Cawley

IVP Books

An imprint of InterVarsity Press
Downers Grove, Illinois

InterVarsity Press
P.O. Box 1400, Downers Grove, IL 60515-1426
ivpress.com
email@ivpress.com

InterVarsity Press® is the book-publishing division of InterVarsity Christian Fellowship/USA®, a movement of students and faculty active on campus at hundreds of universities, colleges and schools of nursing in the United States of America, and a member movement of the International Fellowship of Evangelical Students. For information about local and regional activities, visit intervarsity.org.

All Scripture quotations, unless otherwise indicated, are taken from THE HOLY BIBLE, NEW INTERNATIONAL VERSION®, NIV® Copyright © 1973, 1978, 1984, 2011 by Biblica, Inc.™ Used by permission. All rights reserved worldwide.

While any stories in this book are true, some names and identifying information may have been changed to protect the privacy of individuals.

Cover design: Cindy Kiple
Interior design: Beth McGill
Images: © Bob Vidler/iStockphoto

ISBN 978-0-8308-4450-0 (print)
ISBN 978-0-8308-9968-5 (digital)

Printed in the United States of America ∞

 As a member of the Green Press Initiative, InterVarsity Press is committed to protecting the environment and to the responsible use of natural resources. To learn more, visit greenpressinitiative.org.

Library of Congress Cataloging-in-Publication Data
Names: Cawley, Luke, 1978-
Title: The myth of the non-Christian : engaging atheists, nominal Christians
    and the spiritual but not religious / Luke Cawley.
Description: Downers Grove : InterVarsity Press, 2016. | Includes
    bibliographical references.
Identifiers: LCCN 2015040196 | ISBN 9780830844500 (pbk. : alk. paper)
Subjects: LCSH: Evangelistic work. | Witness bearing (Christianity) |
    Christianity and atheism.
Classification: LCC BV3793 .C39 2016 | DDC 269/.2—dc23
LC record available at http://lccn.loc.gov/2015040196

P   21   20   19   18   17   16   15   14   13   12   11   10   9   8   7   6   5   4   3   2   1

Y   33   32   31   30   29   28   27   26   25   24   23   22   21   20   19   18   17   16

For Mum and Dad,

who first taught me what it means to follow Jesus

through their words and example.

Contents

ONE

Flexibility

there's no such thing as a non-Christian. I am more convinced of this than ever. An atheistic journalist and a hedonistic student helped me understand why. One was crying on the phone, the other was skipping down the street.

THE ATHEIST, CRYING ON THE PHONE

Tabatha's eyes flooded with tears as she spoke on the phone with her mother. She was halfway through a six-week introductory course on Christianity that had thrown her into complete emotional disarray. She had not entered as a questioning atheist, or one who was looking for God. She happily hadn't believed in God, but as a journalist with a sense of curiosity about religion, she had bravely taken the plunge and signed up for the course.

Before Tabatha started she had no particular animus toward religious people. She did, however, think that most religious beliefs were probably "stupid" and that "organized religion is a horrible thing." So she was pleasantly surprised when she found herself liking the Christians who ran the course. They were friendly and welcoming. They were also willing to be open about their struggles and even about personal issues such as their marriages.

By the end of the course she felt uplifted from being among such genuinely happy people. Why, then, was she crying on the phone to

her mother? Was it conviction of sin? An intense sense of her need for
Jesus? Some other great spiritual moment?

No, she was crying because she was frustrated. It saddened, an-
noyed and upset her to be among a group of people who discussed
something as profound as God and yet were unable to satisfactorily
answer her most basic questions about *why* she should place her trust
in him.

Every week she had raised issues such as the trustworthiness of the
Bible, the necessity of believing in God to lead a moral life, the
seeming unfairness of God extending grace to murderers, the scientific
basis for believing in a creator God, the problem of suffering and religion's reputation for perpetuating warfare. And every week the
leaders simply quoted Scripture to her or described her questions as
"something we will never understand."

So she cried. She was sad for the people leading, that they in-
vested their lives in something they had not bothered to think
through or question for themselves. Tabatha probably also cried
because her encounter with Christianity had caused the whole
thing to seem *less* plausible rather than *more* so. She'd hoped for a
different outcome.

In the end, although she had enjoyed making friends through the
course and was conscious of how it had helped others, she decided
that Christianity was not for her. Even if it *were* true, no Christian
seemed able or willing to make a credible case for her accepting it.[1]
So she moved on.

THE HEDONIST, SKIPPING DOWN THE STREET

Not everyone had the same experience as Tabatha. A student named
Karen attended the very same course when it was held in a bar on
a university campus in the north of England. Before joining the
course, Karen was a broken woman. She later said that everything
she had been doing at that time was an attempt to fix herself.
Drinking and attracting male attention were her two favored

methods for attempted self-reparation. Whenever she could persuade a good-looking man to spend time with her, she felt less insecure. Under the surface, though, her anxieties were still there and eventually came back.

God wasn't even on Karen's radar. She hadn't ever given him a second thought and assumed that all religion was a load of rubbish. Who, after all, needs all those rules and regulations? It all seemed so distant from her own struggles. But when two of her university colleagues told her they were launching an introductory course on Christianity, she decided to show them some support. That's how she found herself in a bar talking with a group of Christians.

The people were so friendly and warm, and she found herself increasingly excited about going back. The weekly gathering was like a warm oasis in the midst of her otherwise troubled and turbulent life. She also began to understand that Christianity wasn't anything like her previous assumptions about religion; it was, instead, about a relationship with this very compelling person called Jesus.

On the last night of the course someone from a local church came and spoke about the Holy Spirit. After the speaker finished, music filled the room, and a leader invited the people present to sing along. As Karen stood, listening to the singing, she became open for the first time to the possibility of knowing God. At that very moment a woman approached Karen and offered to pray for her. Karen agreed. The woman placed her hands on Karen and began speaking, and Karen suddenly felt light and happy. The weight of her burdens and insecurities dissolved as she welcomed God into her life.

At the end of the evening she found herself smiling uncontrollably and skipping excitedly across campus and back to her home. She knew she didn't have to fix herself any more. She no longer required the attention of men in order to bolster her self-esteem. Drinking was now unnecessary for her to unlock her confidence. It was the beginning of a life with God that has continued to flourish over the years since.

Two young women attend the exact same course. One becomes convinced that Christianity has no answers and cries on the phone to her mother. The other one senses that Jesus is her only hope and ends up skipping joyfully across campus. Same input, different outcomes.

NO NON-CHRISTIANS

Much of my current ministry with the organization Chrysolis is focused on developing communicators who can speak clearly and persuasively about Jesus in nonchurch settings such as universities, bars and places of business. Prior to that I spent years developing missional communities on university campuses with the International Fellowship of Evangelical Students movement. In both settings it has been common, after I give a talk to Christians, for someone to ask me, "How can we better engage non-Christians with the message of Jesus?" It's always a question that throws me.

Don't get me wrong; I'm all in favor of rethinking how we effectively introduce people to Jesus. But I am a little hazy as to what is meant by a "non-Christian." Does it refer to someone, like Karen, who has a deep emotional longing for personal healing but little concern for the big intellectual issues surrounding religion? Or might it refer to a person, like Tabatha, who needs detailed and considered answers to their complex philosophical and historical questions?

"Non-Christian" is a category so broad it is obsolete. It's not even something people call themselves. Some people I know describe themselves in terms of their sporting allegiances ("Packers fan"), their political affiliation ("libertarian"), their hobbies ("avid reader," "snowboarder") or their relationships ("devoted husband," "struggling parent"). Some might even employ religiously themed labels like "atheist," "secular Jew," "spiritual but not religious" or "vaguely Hindu." I've rarely met anybody, though, who calls himself a "non-Christian."

It's strange, then, that we Christians persist in treating the label as if it were somehow rich with meaning. Perhaps the time has come to retire the term and to rediscover the rich variety that exists among people who are not yet following Jesus.

Not everybody is the same. Our approaches to sharing Jesus should therefore not treat people as such. We need to move from having *a* strategy for communicating with all people to having *multiple* strategies for different groups:

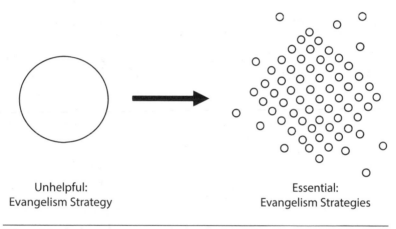

Unhelpful:
Evangelism Strategy

Essential:
Evangelism Strategies

Figure 1.1

Let's think about Tabatha's situation again. There is nothing innately wrong with the course material and format she encountered. It has been used to bring thousands to faith in Christ. Even she enjoyed the friendships. But imagine for a moment what would have happened if the course leaders had redesigned or tweaked the content to specifically address Tabatha. They probably didn't know a great deal about her, but suppose they had made some changes based on these three very basic facts about her, which would have emerged quite early upon meeting her:

She is an atheist.

She is a journalist.

She is a Brit.

Their very rudimentary understanding of Tabatha could be depicted like this:

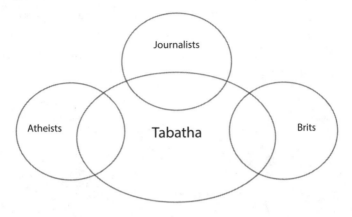

Figure 1.2

You can see from this diagram that no single category completely summarizes everything about Tabatha. And not everything about each group is even true of her personally. But while none of these groups is homogeneous, members of each one tend to have certain things in common. The course leaders could have made the simple observations that:

- Atheists don't believe there is a God. Therefore they will need to address the question of God's existence at some point.

- Brits are citizens of a highly secularized nation and are likely to consider atheism "neutral." The leaders will therefore need to do more than present the case for Christianity; they should also ask some hard questions of the alternatives (including atheism).

- Journalists are accustomed to sorting and assessing evidence. Any discussion of God will therefore need to include an opportunity to grapple with the best evidence for the existence of God and to ask hard questions.

These adjustments wouldn't have guaranteed Tabatha would become a follower of Jesus. That still would have been between her and God. But perhaps she could have come to her decision without the misapprehension that her questions were unanswerable.

Perhaps it would have been difficult to tailor the whole course for journalists—or even atheists—unless they formed a sizable proportion of those present. But the course's small group discussions could easily have been organized so that participants with similar concerns were wrestling with their questions together. This would have created an opportunity for Tabatha to spend more time talking through, for example, the evidence for God. One of the course leaders could even have arranged to go for a drink with Tabatha and discuss her specific queries. She might have come away with a sense that there is a plausible basis for trusting Jesus. Perhaps she would then have continued her investigation of him.

The more we understand the different groups within a culture, the more appropriate our communication of Jesus can become when we encounter someone from those groups. It is not a substitute for getting to know people as individuals. The case of Tabatha shows, though, that reflection on even the simplest things we know about a person makes a difference.

CONTEXTUAL APOLOGETICS

The art of formulating appropriate and diverse ways of sharing Jesus, based on a thorough understanding of those with whom we are interacting, is one that has a rich history within Christianity. Strangely, though, even some fantastically gifted Christian communicators manage to overlook its importance.

A while back I heard a story about one of the top university evangelists in Britain. We'll call him Charlie. He has a long track record of success and several popular books to his name. I respect him greatly, both for his passion and for his personal integrity. A few years ago Charlie was invited by a group of Christian students to spend a week on a university campus in my area. The students organized a series of lunchtime events and evening gatherings in conjunction

with Charlie's talks, which outlined the message of Jesus and addressed major objections to the Christian faith.

At the time of this event a book had just been published called *The
God Delusion*, by Richard Dawkins, which was stirring up debate on
campuses around the country. The book addressed questions such as
whether a belief in God was intellectually tenable or morally desirable.
Charlie used most of his talks to tackle the erroneous arguments of
The God Delusion. He addressed the book's perspective on science and
religion, on Christianity and violence, and on the possibility that faith
was simply psychological self-deception. It was great stuff, humbly
presented, complete with good humor and illustrations. If someone
like Tabatha had been there, I'm sure he or she would have loved it.
Strangely, though, attendance at these events plummeted as the week
went on. Nobody became a follower of Jesus that week. It took a great
deal of convincing for the Christians on campus to run a similar outreach effort again.

When I heard this story, I began wondering why this had happened.
How could such a great speaker as Charlie fail so spectacularly?

I asked the university chaplain, Benedict Cambridge, this question.
Benedict gave me a simple answer: Charlie hadn't understood the
context. Yes, *The God Delusion* had been inspiring debates on many
campuses around the nation, but almost nobody at this particular university had heard of the book, let alone read it. Students there took
classes focused on activity rather than philosophical reflection. Even
when they did engage with the kinds of questions discussed in *The God
Delusion*, they only did so in the classroom. Their main interests
outside lecture hours were making friends, partying and hooking up.
Charlie had given a great series of talks, Benedict affirmed, but they
were just not right for this setting.

Charlie had gone one step better than the people running Tabatha's
course. He had, at least, attempted to meaningfully address major
concerns about the Christian faith. Unfortunately they weren't the
concerns of his audience.

His actions were not an isolated incident. They reflect a dynamic that is quite widespread in the Christian church—a separation between these two important disciplines:

| Contending for the Christian faith in the face of major objections | Understanding the context and reshaping practice accordingly |

Figure 1.3

It's not a division that has taken place intentionally or as the result of any heated arguments. Instead it seems that different groups of people have latched on to the importance of each of these two emphases and have developed a body of expertise and a set of practices around it. The two emphases even have technical names to describe them. The art of commending and defending the Christian faith is called "apologetics." The term comes from a Greek word, *apologia*, meaning "a defense" or "a demonstration of the correctness of an argument or belief."[2] The practice of reflecting on a context and translating the entirety of life and faith accordingly is called "contextual missiology," or "contextualization."

| Apologetics | Contextualization |

Figure 1.4

We need to begin cross-breeding the two disciplines. Their hybrid child, which I like to call "contextual apologetics," combines the strengths of both its parents. It blends contextual awareness with an apologetic emphasis on contending for the plausibility of the Christian faith. Each of these emphases are frequently used to the exclusion of the other, but used together they can have an incredible combined effect.

BREAKING STEREOTYPES

Many Christians picture an apologist as somebody, like the university speaker I mentioned, who has amazing answers to questions few are asking, a person who rattles a sword of logical argumentation at all who draw near. Certainly some apologists fit that description. I hope, though, that this book will give you a fresh perspective on apologetics and open you up to its possibilities within your own life and situation. When apologetics is harnessed to contextual sensitivity it can become quite powerful. It certainly was when I gave my last apologetic talk.

APOLOGETICS IN THE EARLY CHURCH

When Paul visits Thessalonica in Acts, he and his team plant a thriving church in just a few weeks. Paul is described during this trip as "explaining" about Jesus (Acts 17:3). But something more than explanation also occurs. Paul is also recorded as "reasoning" and "proving" that Jesus died and rose from the dead in such a way that his audience eventually become "persuaded" (Acts 17:2-4). He is evidently making a case for the trustworthiness of what he has "explained." He, unlike Tabatha's course leaders, never responds to big issues by saying "just have faith" or "it's a mystery."

I was asked to speak at a Christmas event in a juvenile prison and found myself alone in the middle of an open area surrounded on all sides by cells. Some of the inmates stared down at me from the balconies above. Others sat very close to me and poured all their effort into looking as indifferent as possible. Many stayed in their cells and were hidden behind thick metal doors with just a letter-box-sized window of reinforced glass through which to stare. When I lifted the microphone to my mouth and began to speak, everybody else in the room raised their voices in response. My words hit a wall of noise, and I pushed hard against it. I was determined to be heard. I began to tell them a story about the worst Christmas of my life, when I felt lonely and far from friends and family, wondering whether God even cared about me.

An aggressive voice thundered from one of the cells above, "Shut up! Who cares?"

I turned to the cell and shouted back, "That was exactly *my* question: Who does care?"

The noise didn't subside, but more people seemed to be paying attention now.

I told them that I had given up on God but then read in a book that Jesus said "whoever has seen me has seen the Father." I explained that this meant Jesus was claiming that if you want to know what God is like you should look at him. I then asked them whether they knew the story of Jesus. There was no response. So I said, "Let me tell you some of the basics."

Then something strange happened. As the next section of my talk began, a stillness and silence fell over the room. This is what I said:

> When Jesus was born, there were rumors his mum was a cheap woman who got knocked up by some random guy. He had to live all his life with people making comments about that.
>
> When he was very young the government where he lived decided to have all the kids murdered in his town. The king had some theory about a kid being born who would threaten his power, so he sent the army in to murder the babies. As mothers screamed all through town watching their children die, Jesus and his parents somehow escaped.
>
> He spent years living in a foreign country. He was the weird immigrant kid. Different skin, different language, different food. Everyone looked at him weird. When he eventually moved back to his own country, things were quiet for a while. Then when he was a teenager or maybe in his twenties his dad died. He was left to look after his mum. Be the man of the house. He didn't ask for this.

He got older. Became well known. Did some lovely stuff like healing sick people, telling corrupt powerful people where to get off, looking after poor people.

But the corrupt powerful people didn't like this. They paid one of his best friends to rat him out. This friend got him arrested. All his other friends disappeared. They didn't want anything to do with him now.

One of them used to say he would happily die with Jesus. Now he was telling everyone he never even knew him. What kind of friends were these? He had a trial, which was frankly a pack of lies. People made things up about him. He was misrepresented. Where were his friends now?

Then he was murdered. Stripped naked, nailed to a piece of wood and hung out to die in public.

No dad. No friends. No justice. Nothing. Not even his life.

It was this person. Jesus. Who said that God was like *him*.

And so when I read that, I thought, "Yeah, if that's God, maybe I do want to know him. Maybe I want to give it another shot to connect with him. Because maybe there is somebody out there who is not only bigger than me but is like Jesus. Who knows what it's like to be in the kind of dark place I am in right now."

And that's Christmas. At Christmas we sing and talk about baby Jesus because we think that he was God become a human being. And he shows us God: not a God who is out there and can't understand what it's like to be you. But a God who gets it. Understands. And is worth your while taking seriously.

It was clear as I spoke these words that the teenage inmates were hearing the story of Jesus in relatable form for the first time in their short lives.

This event was powerful partly because it fused apologetics with contextual sensitivity. I wanted to establish the story of Jesus as a live option for those who might otherwise dismiss it as irrelevant. This was apologetics. But I did so by telling the story in a way that related to the realities of my listener's lives. This was contextualization. The combination—contextual apologetics—is so potent it can silence a rowdy prison.

WIDENING OUR VIEW OF APOLOGETICS

Renowned apologist John Stackhouse writes that "anything that helps people take Christianity more seriously than they did before, anything that helps defend and commend it, properly counts as apologetics."[3] The word *anything* is the key. It's not just about making detailed logical arguments. It also includes approaches like telling stories well and crafting song lyrics that grab the imagination of our listeners.

Jesus the Contextual Apologist

Jesus' life and actions provide the template for contextual apologetics. Jesus didn't just study the context; he became part of it. He added humanity to his divinity, and not just a generic version of being human. He chose one rooted in a specific time and place. He spoke Hebrew, attended synagogue, worked in the building trade as a carpenter, wore a tunic and ate kosher food. In a world before toothpaste he probably sometimes had bad breath, and in an age without hair dryers it is unlikely he had the blow-dried hair of the actors who play him in movies.

Since Jesus lived in a culture distant to our own, we often mistakenly assume that everything he did and said was original to him. It wasn't. Part of Jesus' genius lay in the way he took things that already existed and used them in fresh ways. Parables, for example, were used for thousands of years before Jesus started telling them.[4] The man from Nazareth, though, took this ancient art form and used it to say things we are still quoting thousands of years later.

One of these parables is about two men (Lk 18:9-14). The first (a Pharisee) is a very upright, religious person, and the second (a tax collector) is a corrupt and immoral one. The first man starts praying and sneaks a condescending glance at the other man. He reels off a list of achievements and thanks God for his own awesomeness. He praises the Lord he is not like this awful chap over here. His entire prayer is about himself.

Switch focus to man number two. His prayer is much briefer. He can only hang his head in shame and say, "God, have mercy on me, a sinner." That's all he has. No list of achievements. Just a pathetic confession. They both go home, and Jesus pulls out the twist in the tale: it is the second man and not the first who arrives at his house accepted by God.

This is a familiar story for many Christians. You may even think you already know the story. But reflect on it again. It is much more clever than it seems on the surface. It doesn't just tell us something; it does something to us. I once heard about a Sunday school teacher who taught this parable to her class. She concluded her lesson by saying, "And let's thank God we aren't like the Pharisee."

Do you see what happened with this teacher? Reading that story exposed her tendency to act exactly like the Pharisee. She couldn't interact with the parable without judging its villain, and so her likeness to him became apparent.

And when you read the story about the Sunday school teacher, what went through your mind? Did you look down on her because you would never make her obvious mistake? Maybe you turn out to be like the Pharisee too.

This is Jesus' genius. He tells what seems like a simple story and yet, as you encounter it, you find your own self-righteousness coaxed gently out into the open. You aren't just told about your sin. You are almost provoked to enact the very transgression he is discussing. Such are the shock waves it creates that you can't even read about somebody else's response to the parable without uncovering your inner Pharisee.

This is contextual apologetics at its best: convincing and persuading the listener by using forms and methods appropriate to the setting. Jesus didn't invent parables. He wasn't the first person to talk about temples, Pharisees, tax collectors or prayer. But he brought all those familiar elements together in a way that makes the truth about our own sin inescapable.

Jesus was an apologist who sought to convince others of what he was saying. He did so through inventive use of the contextually familiar means of parables. The outcome was compelling, sometimes devastating. Nobody who listened carefully was left unconvinced, and they either had to follow him or violently silence him.

APOLOGETICS IS FOR EVERYONE

It's not just speakers and church leaders who need to be able to outline *why* Jesus can be trusted. Peter, in the New Testament, writes to a group of ordinary first-century Jesus followers that they also need to "always be prepared to give an answer to everyone who asks you to give the reason for the hope that you have" (1 Pet 3:15). As our interaction with others gives rise to questions, Peter is saying, we will *all* need to provide thoughtful and persuasive responses.

THREE KEY GROUPS OF PEOPLE

In this book we will follow in Jesus' footsteps by learning to be contextual apologists in our own settings. We will meet three sets of people:

- The "spiritual but not religious"
- Convinced atheists
- Nominal Christians

These groups include the majority of the people not following Jesus in the West today. Here's why:[5]

71% of the US population
describe themselves as "Christian"

39% of the US population
attend church on a weekly basis[6]

The details of how these two figures relate can be debated. Some churchgoers are obviously not true followers of Jesus, while some followers of Jesus may not currently be involved regularly in a local fellowship. But however you slice it, it is clear that many people outside the church—about a third of the US population—self-identify as "Christian" despite not being active in a community where they can learn and grow in their professed faith. These millions of people include many of the "nominal Christians" we will be considering later in this book.

Here's another striking statistic:

23% of the US population
are religiously unaffiliated

37% of the religiously
unaffiliated in the US describe
themselves as "spiritual"[7]

That means (to save you the math!) that around 8 percent of US adults see themselves as "spiritual" but do not embrace any formal religion. That's why I chose to focus partly on the spiritual but not religious; they include a full third of those who would not call themselves "Christian."

> ## NOT FROM THE UNITED STATES?
>
> Check out appendix one, which provides equivalent statistics for Canada and the United Kingdom.

Atheists are still quite a small segment within US society. However, they are a group that garners much media exposure and is also growing quite substantially:

4.0% of the US population identified as "atheist" or "agnostic" in 2007

7.1% of the US population identified as "atheist" or "agnostic" in 2014

So learning to engage with the three groups discussed in this book will aid you in your conversations and interactions with a significant percentage of people around you.

We will learn to be contextual apologists among these three sets of people. As we meet each group, we will hear their stories and begin to better understand them for ourselves. Each set of people is diverse, and we will note both the differences *within* each category and also their defining *common features*. Such in-depth listening is foundational to good apologetics and also to effective contextualization. Chapters four, seven and ten are the ones that focus on this intensive understanding of context.

After meeting each set of people, we will begin to listen to their questions and misgivings about the Christian faith. We'll also think through some of the most helpful answers and responses to address those concerns. No one answer will satisfy everybody, but having an awareness of some possible lines of response to major issues will enable us to be more helpful conversation partners to people in these three groups. Chapters five, eight and eleven deal most directly with formulating such responses and are the most apologetically slanted sections of the book.

ADAPTATION: PART OF THE CHRISTIAN DNA

Think about the last church meeting you attended. Was it in English, Spanish or maybe Korean? One thing's for certain: it wasn't in Aramaic, even though that was likely the language in which Jesus did most of his original teaching. Nor was it in ancient Greek, the language of the New Testament.

Almost all contemporary Christians practice a faith translated from its original linguistic and cultural roots. Adaption and flexibility seem to be written into the DNA of the Christian movement. In part this is a reflection of God's nature. He is diverse (Father, Son and Spirit) and also harmonious (one God). Diversity is therefore intrinsic to God's very being. He intends his world and also his church to echo his own trinitarian nature by being unified and yet varied.

In addition to considering possible responses to specific questions, we will also discuss various practices that can help us more appropriately engage people with the story of Jesus. We will learn to change the form of our evangelism and not just the words we use. Jesus used parables. What should we do with atheists, nominal Christians and people who consider themselves spiritual? Chapters six, nine and twelve offer a few ideas. Each one focuses on a series of interviews with some of today's best evangelistic practitioners. They share stories and advice that will help us better approach our own unique settings.

Before we begin exploring these different contexts, though, we'll delve a little more into some aspects of apologetics and contextualization that are helpful across a range of settings. You'll find out more about these in the next two chapters. They offer an alternative way of practicing apologetics to the currently popular ones, which focus solely on logic or on engaging with worldviews.

After reading the first three chapters, feel free to skip to the sections that interest you the most. This table may help you to visualize the structure of the book:

Table 1.1

	Spiritual But Not Religious ⇩	Convinced Atheists ⇩	Nominal Christians ⇩
Good approaches for all contexts ⇨	chapters one, two, three and thirteen		
Understanding the specific context we are engaging ("stories") ⇨	chapter four	chapter seven	chapter ten
Responding to the major questions in this context ("questions") ⇨	chapter five	chapter eight	chapter eleven
Developing practices specifically helpful to this context ("practices") ⇨	chapter six	chapter nine	chapter twelve

YOUR SETTING

There must be people who you wish would take the story of Jesus more seriously: friends, neighbors, family members or work mates. Maybe you are intensely conscious that your current models of communicating about Jesus are not quite right for these particular people. Perhaps you've begun to wonder whether either you or your Christian community could ever effectively engage with them.

If so, then it's time to think again. Just because you or your community have not previously introduced Jesus in contextually appropriate ways doesn't mean you can't start right now. There are ways to engage people with his story that can bring peace to a prison and open hostile people up to appreciating his beauty for the first time. We can reach both Tabatha *and* Karen, as well as a host of other people.

It starts as we discard the myth of a generic "non-Christian" and begin to grapple with the diversity of people and questions that exist all around us.

Taking It Further

Here's an easy way to get thinking about people you know: Write the name of someone in the large middle circle below. In the smaller overlapping circles write some important aspects of that person. Then spend a few minutes reflecting, praying and making notes on the implications of this for how you might introduce them to Jesus:

Notes:

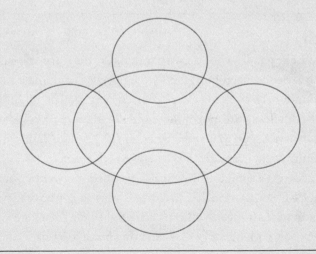

Figure 1.5

TWO

Plausibility & Desirability

e ven contextually sensitive apologetics can easily go wrong. This has happened in my own experience. Discovering apologetics, in fact, led to my most unfruitful period of ministry. It all began when I woke up on my first Christmas Day morning as an overseas missionary and found I had accidentally become an atheist.

FROM MISSIONARY TO ATHEIST . . .

I was as startled by this development as anybody else. I'd grown up in a strong Christian family in the UK and had come to my adult experience of faith through a combination of charismatic prayer meetings and a homeless man approaching me on the street with an unsolicited word of prophecy. The day after opening my life to Jesus I was preaching to a feisty crowd of Muslims in central London. Spiritual experience and passionate activism, then, have always featured prominently in my life as a Christian.

By the age of twenty-two I had moved to Bucharest, Romania, to work with a university campus ministry. It was here that the first cracks began to show. The greatest points of tension occurred on a bench and a bus.

The bench was a simple wooden one nestled among the trees. It looked out over a lake near my Bucharest apartment and was hidden enough for me to spend a couple of hours a day there praying. It should have been an idyllic spot. Instead it was a place of frustration. I was increasingly struggling with the question of how to have a relationship with someone who is invisible. Trying to connect with God was like attempting to hug a cloud. It was lonely being so far from home, and I had expected an overwhelming sense of God's presence while serving as a missionary in Romania. Instead God seemed distant. I began to wonder whether he was even there or, if he was, whether he actually cared about me.

When I left the bench I would get on a bus. A man with no legs would regularly work his way through its central aisle asking for money. His reddened stumps were festering and protected only by bits of leather tied on with brown string. In each hand he held a metal doorhandle screwed to a small square of wood. He used these as substitute feet and swung himself though the vehicle with his hands pushing down on the door handles. I'd heard that he was placed on the railway line by his parents as a child, so that his legs could be severed and he could make more money as a beggar.

Every time I got off the bus, I would pass a group of street children who lived in the sewers, having fled there to escape abusive parents. They would approach me in their ragged and filthy clothes asking for money. I tried to carry sandwiches with me in my bag and would give them some. Every time I left them, though, I would feel deeply unsettled by what I had witnessed. Where was God in all this? Wasn't he supposed to be good? How, then, could he look down and not do anything? For all my passion and activism I had never been so brutally confronted by intellectual and emotional challenges to my faith. My sense of God's absence increased. Visits to the bench became more infrequent, and eventually they ceased altogether.

Finally, on Christmas Day morning, I woke up and uttered the oddest prayer of my life. I said "God, I don't think you exist. And if you do, then I don't think I like you." It was an honest prayer and also felt like a significant one. A weight seemed to lift from my shoulders, and I was taking my first steps into the brave new God-free world. I had moved from missionary to atheist. I was confronting the reality of suffering and choosing the only sensible way of addressing it.

Within the course of just three months I had managed to take an unexpected path from passionate young missionary to one who found the possibility of God untenable. What happened next, though, surprised me even further.

. . . AND BACK AGAIN

It took only a few hours for me to discover that I had solved nothing. Later that Christmas Day I left my apartment, and the street children were still begging and living rough. I got on the bus, and the legless man was still there. That's when it hit me: even if you get rid of God, suffering is still a problem. It's an issue whether you are Christian or not.

After I got off the bus that Christmas Day, I went to some friends' house, and they gave me a parcel that had come for me in the post. I opened it and found a book. It had a nice cover with a silhouette of Jesus on it, and I began thinking about how much I liked Jesus. I struggled with the idea of God. But I liked Jesus. He's someone with whom I would have enjoyed spending time. We could have been friends.

I opened the book and began reading. For the first time I came across the quotation from Jesus I cited in the prison talk from the last chapter. It read: "Anyone who has seen me has seen the Father" (Jn 14:9). If you want to know what God is like, in other words, look at the life and character of Jesus.

It was as though someone had switched the lights on in my brain. I saw for the first time that God was not distant or "looking down" on suffering. He has suffered with us and for us. Jürgen Moltmann, in a lecture I heard years later, suggested that the starting point for all discussion of God should be a bleeding man nailed to a wooden cross.[1] Yale philosopher Nicholas Wolterstorff, reflecting on the loss of his own son in a climbing accident, writes of how the life of Christ had highlighted this perspective on God:

We're in it together, God and we, together in the history of our
world. The history of the world is the history of our suffering
together. Every act of evil extracts a tear from God, every plunge
into anguish extracts a sob from God.[2]

This rediscovery of the suffering God didn't resolve every question
I had about the subject—*many* (though not all) of those were addressed though books I read over subsequent months—but it was the
dawn of my realization that Christianity has compelling responses to
the biggest questions and doubts we can throw its way. More than this,
though, it also highlighted for me that Jesus brings clarity to the most
profound questions that everybody, Christian or otherwise, has about
life. It was the birth of my passion for apologetics.

Soon I found myself returning to the bench. In my pocket was a
New Testament. Each day I would read a short section from Jesus' life
and then speak to God as if he had the personality and character of
Jesus. This became more than a psychological exercise. It actually
opened the door to God, as I found that the person about whom I was
reading was the very one I had been reaching for all these months. He,
in fact, had already been reaching out to me.

My hardest doubts since my conversion had done their worst. But they
hadn't won. What drew me back from the gates of atheism was the discovery that Jesus could make sense of even my most confusing questions.

ENTER THE APOLOGIST

My experience of briefly swerving into atheism, and back out again,
began to reshape my work among university students in Bucharest.
Until this period of crisis, my public speaking had only taken the form
of biblical expositions. These had been quite fruitful, and people were
regularly drawn to Christ through them. But I wondered whether
some of the students were in the same situation I had been and were
wrestling with major doubts. So I began integrating little fragments
of apologetics into my presentations.

More than a year passed until I was able to dedicate an entire talk to addressing a major difficulty with the Christian faith. The occasion was an Easter event at which many newcomers were expected. My flatmate alone was bringing seven of his colleagues. I decided this was a great chance to tackle the question of whether the resurrection really happened. I'd been reading many books on the topic and was amazed by how strongly the historical evidence pointed toward Jesus having physically risen from the dead. So my entire half-hour presentation focused on this topic.

But weirdly enough, even as I was speaking I could feel my talk falling flat. People looked restless and bored. I was used to seeing audiences moved, gripped, sometimes crying. Rarely had I witnessed so many eyes glancing down at watches and phones to check the passing time. Nobody approached me to talk afterwards. When I returned home my flatmate told me how disappointed he was in what his friends had heard. "I expected something powerful like you normally present," he told me, "but instead you brought all this philosophy and history." His friends had not felt any impact from my talk, and he felt as though an opportunity had been missed.

I was surprised by this outcome, but I didn't panic. It was my first attempt at this kind of presentation, and it was bound to be a learning process. As I engaged in postgame analysis with my friends about the talk, I came to a conclusion that later proved to be only half accurate: I had picked the wrong question in my Easter presentation. The issue of the resurrection is not one that vexes most students in nominally Eastern Orthodox Romania. They generally take for granted the possibility of such an event. What I needed to do instead was address some of the objections to Christianity that they do actually hold. There is no such thing as a generic "non-Christian," and I needed to start practicing better contextual apologetics.

As a result of this experience, I became better at understanding and responding to the major objections of each given context in which I spoke. When I later found myself in a new role launching and developing student-led missional communities on college campuses, the students and I created lunchtime and evening events focused around the hot topics of the day and the most common objections to the Christian faith. These events were quite successful. New people would attend, engage with the questions being discussed and leave, saying, "Yes, I definitely think Christianity could be true." This was a good outcome. But it was accompanied by a worrisome trend: very few of the people attending these meetings were actually starting to follow Jesus for themselves.

FAITH VS. EVIDENCE?

Jesus told Thomas, who struggled to believe in the resurrection until he saw him with his own eyes, "Because you have seen me, you have believed; blessed are those who have not seen and yet have believed" (Jn 20:29).

Many wrongly assume that Jesus here is recommending we believe things for which there is no evidence. But this isn't the point Jesus is making.

He is instead drawing a contrast between Thomas, who was able to gaze on the risen Jesus, and subsequent generations of believers who would have to rely on forms of evidence other than visual and physical encounters with Christ.[3]

Even John, who wrote down the encounter between Jesus and Thomas, says he has "written that you may believe" (Jn 20:31). My former professor John Lennox comments that John, in this verse, is explicitly stating his intent "that what he is writing [about Jesus] is to be part of the evidence on which faith is based."[4]

Lennox adds that "it is no part of the biblical worldview that things should be believed when there is no evidence."[5]

It seemed that I had become adept at demonstrating the *plausibility* of the Christian faith, but I was utterly failing to establish that it was also *desirable*. Newcomers could therefore see that Christianity might be true, but they didn't view it as something they personally wanted to pursue. My approach needed to change.

WHAT I FORGOT

I was not alone in focusing only on questions of plausibility. Most apologetic books and talks do the same thing. They try to establish the credibility of basic Christian teachings in the face of common objections.

This is a necessary task. Few will be open to embracing something that is blatantly not true. Plausibility matters to almost everybody. But it just isn't enough. Plausibility is like a safety net that adds confidence. But it isn't compelling. Perhaps, in decades past, seeing that something could be true automatically led to people being interested in it. Plausibility established desirability. Now, though, plausibility and desirability have widely become uncoupled from each other. Truth is no longer cherished in quite the same way. Demonstrating the trustworthiness of something is no longer sufficient to arouse interest. It merely prevents people from dismissing it out of hand.

The question, then, is how we can invoke desire. I wrestled constantly with this problem after I realized that our campus-based events weren't working quite as I wished. The turning point eventually came for me when I was speaking at a series of large outreach events at another university far from where I lived. The first night I was asked to speak to several hundred people about the reliability of Scripture. My twenty-five-minute talk went smoothly, and I covered all the essentials of textual reliability and historical veracity. Afterwards there was half an hour of questions from the audience. People asked thoughtful questions, but they seemed mostly to have been drawn from the outlandish ideas contained in Dan Brown's bestseller *The Da Vinci Code*. Nobody asked a single question indicating that they had ever actually read the Bible. Afterwards, as I wandered back to my accommodations, I wondered whether I might have been better advised to simply encourage people to read Scripture for themselves.

A few months later I was invited to speak at a similar event. This time I altered my approach and spent just three minutes of my talk discussing the authenticity of the New Testament documents. The rest of the time I showed art inspired by the life of Jesus, highlighted social movements motivated by his example, shared the story of Jesus' work in my life and finished by asking my listeners to pause and imagine for themselves what it might mean if Jesus was right when he said, "I am the light of the world. Whoever follows me will never walk in darkness, but will have the light of life" (Jn 8:12).

I then challenged them to read the life of Jesus for themselves with open minds. Afterwards, many people—none of them Christians—came up to me and excitedly told me how much they had enjoyed my presentation. They were each gripping one of the copies of the Gospel of Luke we had left on tables around the room and enthusiastically assured me that they intended to go away and read it for themselves. It was a noticeable change from the normal nodding of agreement that I might be right.

Shortly after this I realized exactly why my change of approach had so much impact. I was preparing a talk on suffering and started thinking back over the crisis of faith I'd experienced back in Romania. It struck me that the defining aspect of that period was my realization that we live in a universe created and sustained by the crucified God. It was the person of Jesus who had most decisively made Christianity both plausible and desirable to me in the face of the hard questions I was asking.

Jesus was also the focus of my new, adjusted approach to addressing the issue of whether we can trust the New Testament. I'd shared some of his story from the Gospels, spoken of his work in my life and highlighted his impact throughout human history. And people had been affected. Perhaps, I surmised, Jesus should begin to take center stage again as I sought to help others with the whole range of their concerns and doubts.

Recentering my communication around Jesus helped me to overcome an impasse in my outreach efforts. I didn't abandon issues of plausibility and factuality. But they ceased to be my focus.

ARGUING FROM JESUS

Making Jesus integral to our apologetics is not simply a pragmatic move. It reflects New Testament priorities. Paul, when writing to the Corinthian church, summarizes the principle theme of his communication in this way: "For I resolved to know nothing while I was with you except Jesus Christ and him crucified" (1 Cor 2:2).

Note that he cites two aspects to his message: a person ("Jesus Christ") and an event ("him crucified"). Frequently, when Paul mentions the cross, he is using it as shorthand for the entire Easter event, including the resurrection. Paul says that his focus was this person and the climatic days of his earthly life.

My apologetics went wrong because I began viewing the treatment of life's big questions as a separate discipline from the kind of ordinary Christian communication described by Paul. You might say that I had allowed *apologetics* to become estranged from *evangelism*. When I addressed major objections to the Christian faith it was as if I were walking people down a dead-end street. They found answers to their questions there, but no through road to encountering Jesus for themselves. It was therefore inevitable that fewer people would begin following him.

I wasn't alone in this regard. One well-known apologist does exactly the same thing. This lauded academic and author was invited to speak on a university campus near me and gave a compelling argument for the existence of God. He used science and philosophy to make his case. After the event I asked a colleague for his take on what we'd heard. He paused in thought for a moment. "It was convincing," he told me, "but to be honest, a Muslim could have given that talk. He certainly showed there may be a God. But you have no idea what his God is like, and you certainly feel no sense of being drawn to him." My friend's words were like a dagger to me because although I am much less talented than this great apologist, I was nevertheless in danger of falling into the very same trap.

I decided to instead follow Paul's example of focusing on the person of Jesus and the concluding events of his life on earth. This didn't mean abandoning an apologetic practice of helping people wrestle through their questions about Jesus. But I needed to change *how* I did so. My new approach had two dimensions:

Arguing *from*
Arguing *toward* **Jesus**

Figure 2.1

Arguing *from* Jesus is a very simple practice. It involves, in conversations and in talks, highlighting how Jesus and/or the Easter event might be relevant to the question in hand. Jesus, as was earlier highlighted, called himself "the light of the world." Light is not something you look *at* so much as it is something you look *with*. C. S. Lewis famously compared his discovery of Jesus with a sunrise and noted that he knows the sun has risen "not only because I see it, but because by it I see everything else."[6] We can help our friends see the desirability of Jesus by leaning on his capacity to illuminate all of life, including their doubts and questions.

My confrontation with the question of suffering is one example of how this works in practice. It was through a rediscovery of Jesus' claim to divinity, read in light of his incarnated life and bloody death, that I began to make sense of the brokenness around me.

Similarly illuminating encounters could be repeated in a range of situations. Consider, for example, a person who says that they dislike Christianity due to hypocritical behavior they have experienced within the church. You could sympathize and say, "Some of Jesus' harshest criticisms were aimed at phony religious leaders. He said they were like beautifully painted graves, attractive on the outside but rotting on the inside. I think he'd agree with you on this one." It's a simple response that draws *from* the life of Jesus to highlight to your conversation partner that disappointment with the church doesn't put them at odds with Jesus. Their criticisms actually echo ones that passed through his own lips.

Sometimes, though, a discussion doesn't afford the opportunity to readily speak *from* the person of Jesus or the Easter event. Doing so would be forced and unnatural. This is where we argue *toward* Jesus. He may not be the main topic of our conversation, but we do want to highlight how the subject of our discussion can only be resolved through engagement with him.

For instance, you may have met people who reject Christianity because of all the bloodshed, violence and misogyny in the Old Testament. Dealing with this question will require explaining that in terms of genre, much of the Old Testament is history. It tells stories of what occurred. The biblical characters are often not the heroes; in actuality, they constantly make wrong choices.

If necessary, we might then go into details of specific biblical texts that on the surface seem to commend genocide (see appendix two for more on this topic). Pretty soon, though, we will need to say something such as, "The Old Testament gets confusing for me too, but Christians tend not to treat it as the best starting point for thinking about God. Instead we begin with the idea that God has made himself known to us through the life of a human being, Jesus, who actually died as the victim of violence."

This is arguing *toward* Jesus. We don't *start* by speaking about his relevance to the issue. Instead we move *toward* highlighting how the discussion can only be resolved through a fresh investigation of him. Jesus is the endpoint of the argument.

Chapters five, eight and eleven of this book (each labeled "Questions") will provide you with more detailed examples of how we can both argue *from* Jesus and also *toward* him. It's a very simple way to strengthen our contextual apologetics by responding uniquely to each person's given concerns while also allowing the desirable Jesus to have a voice in the conversation.

JESUS: OUR BEST ARGUMENT

The best argument for God is the person of Jesus. As philosopher Michael Buckley writes: "One will not long believe in a personal God with whom there is no personal communication, and the most compelling evidence of a personal God must itself be personal."[7] We neuter our potential impact if we push Jesus to the periphery of our communication.

BEYOND REASON

Focusing on Jesus, then, was the key component enabling me to shift from eliciting the agreement of my audiences to provoking their interest and excitement. I made this discovery almost by accident, and yet after doing so I realized I was aligning myself with the early church practice of centering verbal communication on Christ and him crucified. I also became aware that it was Jesus—and not simply arguments about him—who had been central to my own journey away from the fringes of atheism and back toward Christianity.

I learned that apologetics shouldn't be a prelude to communicating about Jesus. He is our strongest argument, and speaking about him—his earthly life, his historical impact over the centuries, his role in our own lives—is crucial if we are to help others see that he is desirable.

TAKING IT FURTHER

Are you wondering how to establish desirability and plausibility with your friends? Read slowly through these four questions. Pause after each one to reflect and note your responses.

1. Which objection to Christianity is trickiest for you to answer?

2. How might Jesus be directly relevant to this question? How could you argue from him or toward him when this topic next emerges in conversation?

3. Do you think any less of the author (or of Jesus) after reading about Luke's doubts and questions as a missionary in Romania? Why or why not?

4. Would it enrich or harm your credibility with people outside the church if you were also open about your own doubts and struggles? Why or why not? What are ways you could do so with more intentionality?

THREE

Tangibility

desirability and plausibility are rarely sufficient to help people begin following Jesus. There is a third, often neglected, element in most spiritual journeys. You can begin to understand it by meeting my friend Martin Smith and hearing his tale.

I ONCE WAS A TEENAGE ATHEIST

Martin was a teenage atheist. He'd not grown up around religion. His father had a vague belief that God existed, and his mother, raised atheist in Catholic Spain, rarely spoke of such matters. The only experience he'd had with Christianity came from his Boy Scout Pack meeting in an Anglican church hall and occasional religion lessons at school. Martin says that when he was very young, he probably considered himself "somewhat Christian" due to his British heritage, but that his upbringing was essentially secular.

In his early teens, though, he began to ponder some big questions. He wondered why he existed, whether anything in this world really mattered, and what caused the universe itself to first emerge. Martin probed his nominal understanding of Christianity to see whether it provided any answers. He eventually reached the conclusion that it couldn't be taken seriously, for several reasons: science has done away with the need for God, the New Testament is pure fabrication, and God seems inactive in the face of global suffering. Atheism held limited attraction for him, but Martin reluctantly embraced it because it seemed like the only intellectually tenable option available to him in light of Christianity's patent implausibility.

It was during this time that a close friend invited Martin to attend a church youth group. Martin agreed and soon became a regular. He enjoyed the activities, and though he was occasionally subversive and disruptive throughout his six years of involvement, he was not particularly hostile to the biblical content of the meetings. "The idea of God becoming man and dying for us," Martin later explained, "seemed quite beautiful to me." But he could never embrace it because of his sincere objections about science, Scripture and suffering. He saw the message of Jesus as desirable but implausible.

Throughout his teens, Martin looked like an apologist's dream: a deep thinker who held many of the classic objections to Christianity and yet who would like it to be true. It seemed he simply needed to meet someone who could provide all the answers to his questions. Maybe everything would snowball if he encountered a Christian who could make the desirable Jesus seem plausible.

Things began to change when Martin turned eighteen. Surprisingly, though, the plausibility of Christianity was not what catalyzed the process of dismantling his atheism. Instead, the cause was a close friendship he had formed with the daughter of the church youth group leader. She invited Martin to her family home, and he began to spend time and eat regularly with them. The atmosphere in their house, which he describes as "joyous, communicative and deeply engaged on an interpersonal level," was unlike any he'd previously experienced. Martin says he witnessed "an example of a life which was deeper, richer and qualitatively better" than his own. Christianity wasn't yet plausible to him. But it was rapidly becoming tangible. Regular immersion in an authentically Christian home was making it real enough to touch.

Before long he felt increasingly confident to raise his big questions over dinner with the family. They took his concerns seriously, did their best to respond well and also lent him various relevant books. He discovered that his objections to Christianity were not as well founded as he'd previously assumed. Soon the desirable Jesus, whose transformative power had been made tangible in this family's life, began to also seem plausible.

Martin says that he increasingly began to "think Christianly" and drift toward Jesus. One Sunday evening, two weeks before leaving for college, he was attending the local Pentecostal church with his friend's family. The speaker invited those present to respond to Jesus for themselves by symbolically walking forward to the front of the auditorium. Martin says the Christian song lyric "I dare you to move" flashed through his head.[1] He stood up, put one foot in front of the other and stepped into a new life of following Jesus, which has continued to grow in vibrancy in the years since.

Martin, a deep thinker with firm objections to the Christian faith, had been drawn to Jesus from a considered adherence to atheism. His major questions and concerns about Christianity had been addressed. But the answers he found, though essential to his faith journey, played a less pivotal role than the family who helped Martin to "imaginatively see what it really means to follow Jesus."

BEYOND DESIRE

Enabling others to tangibly sense the reality of Jesus is an indispensable element of contextual apologetics. Our friends, like Martin, need to encounter the message of Jesus in a form and setting that makes it come alive to them. Only then can the desirable and plausible Jesus be seriously considered as someone to whom they might commit their lives.

Even very intellectual individuals such as Martin, who is currently embarking on graduate work at Oxford University, are more than brains in jars. They don't just think. They also emote, touch, talk, eat and walk. It should therefore not surprise us that most journeys to faith will require more than just rational arguments *from* or *toward* Jesus.

Martin discovered Christianity was desirable and tangible *before* he ever saw it as plausible. This is a common motif in many conversion stories. For example, Martin and I have a mutual friend named Tamara. She grew up nominally Roman Catholic, and her occasional church contact gave her intriguing glimpses of the biblical narrative. Tamara longed for there to really be a personal and knowable God. Yet she couldn't get past her big intellectual questions, such as her sense that religion is essentially a psychological construct and her doubt that just one among the many world belief systems could be true.

Like Martin, though, the turning point in Tamara's relationship with God wasn't triggered by encountering reasoned responses to her questions. It instead occurred as she listened to the music of classical composer Gustav Mahler. His sincere lyrical wrestling with life's complex blend of beauty and brokenness is epitomized in lines from his *Symphony no. 2*, which reflects on Jesus' resurrection:

> You were not born in vain,
> Have not lived in vain, suffered in vain!
> What was created must perish,
> What has perished must rise again![2]

She said these words, and the accompanying music made biblical themes feel real for the first time. They resonated with her so deeply, Tamara told me, that she decided "maybe the closest I can get to God is playing in a big orchestra."

Tamara consequently became increasingly absorbed in exploring the divine through music. She also began reading online about God and music, and stumbled across an article by Boston Symphony Orchestra bass trombonist Doug Yeo. The piece, titled "The Puzzle of Our Lives," spoke to her own thinking and experiences.[3] So she sent Yeo, whom she'd never met, an email sharing her story.

Yeo, who is a Christian, replied affirming her thoughtful curiosity. He told her not to check her brain at the door and to "be honest with God; he can handle your questions." So began a correspondence that eventually led to her finding many of the answers to her questions in works Yeo recommended by Christian apologists C. S. Lewis and G. K. Chesterton.

Tamara, like Martin, had deemed Jesus desirable but implausible. But by listening to the music of an honest spiritual seeker, Gustav Mahler, biblical themes became tangible enough for her to shift from vague curiosity to active seeking.[4] Plausibility came afterwards.

AN INTEGRATED APPROACH

The ideal approach to communicating Jesus will bring together all three elements highlighted in Martin's and Tamara's stories:

Table 3.1

	Addresses the Question:	Relies on:
Plausibility	"Is it true?"	Words and arguments
Desirability	"Is it attractive?"	A focus on Jesus
Tangibility	"Is it real?"	Form, setting and relationship

It's a blend with a fine vintage. As far back as the 1600s, the French mathematician Blaise Pascal famously wrote that an apologist's role is to "show that religion is not contrary to reason, but worthy of reverence and respect. Next make it attractive, make good [people] wish it were true, and then show that it is."[5]

He saw, in other words, that one needs plausibility ("not contrary to reason"), desirability ("make it attractive") and tangibility ("show that it is"). This aspect of contextual apologetics is therefore far from novel. Martin and Tamara, however, had these experiences in a different order from that described by Pascal: They "wished" the message of Jesus were true, someone "showed" them it was, *then* they discovered it is "not contrary to reason." Tangibility and desirability preceded plausibility for them. But each played a part.[6]

Tangibility, plausibility and desirability are unique enough to each be categorized and analyzed individually. In practice, though, the borders between them are blurred, and they form part of an organic whole. Each one gives life to the other two.

For example, dinners with the youth group leader's family were not the only things that made life with Jesus tangible to Martin. Answers he found in books he borrowed also had the same effect; through them he saw that Christianity was solid enough to withstand the real-world battering of his own questions. Plausibility helped make Jesus tangible.

The family's attractive inner life, moreover, didn't just make Jesus tangible. It also showed Martin that following Jesus—like following anything or anyone true—works in everyday life and not just in the pages of a book. In other words, the tangibility of the family's walk with God facilitated the plausibility of Martin following Jesus.

Despite the interconnected nature of the three elements, however, it is still helpful to retain them as distinct categories. Doing so helps us better assess our own practice and identify possible blind spots, such as the common mistake of entirely overlooking the importance of tangibility.

The temptation, on recognizing the significance of one of these three elements, is to focus on it to the exclusion of the other two. Apologetics, as a discipline, tends to treat plausibility as the only issue that matters. But most of the things that initially drew Martin to Christ—hospitality, strong family life, warm friendships, conversations over food, vibrant church services with calls to response, and memorable song lyrics—are oddly absent from almost every book or seminar I have ever encountered on the topic of apologetics. These resources seem to assume that a good argument and a humble demeanor are all that one needs in order to be an effective apologist. *Where* and *how* we engage people—the community setting, the geographical location, the music, whether there is food on the table—rarely gets much attention.

This needs to change. Tangibility needs to be rediscovered. It is unusual for an apologist to speak about the role of church community, the place of healing prayer or the need to engage in social action. But you'll find all these things highlighted in later sections of this book.

We must not reduce our interactions with people, even very smart ones, purely to a series of arguments about the basics of Christianity. We will also need to discover ways in which we, like the family that invited Martin into their home, can enable Jesus' reality to take firm shape before others' eyes.

CHURCH & CONTEXTUAL APOLOGETICS

Martin was deeply affected by something as simple as dinner and discussion. The tangibility aspect of contextual apologetics is therefore not primarily about inventing cool new approaches to ministry. It's more about rediscovering fresh ways in which the existing basics of a Christian's life—mealtimes, conversations over coffee, church services, life in the neighborhood—can be recalibrated to help make Christ more concrete to people in our lives who don't know him.

You can undertake these adjustments whatever your church context may be. I am currently a member of a church founded after John Wesley rode into town on horseback in the 1700s. Prior to that I was involved with a brand-new experimental church plant that met in a café-style space in our city's nightclub district. These two experiences have strengthened my conviction that many of the best evangelism practices work in both conventional churches and also in newer, more radical congregations.

But you do have to be willing to make some changes. Leaning on established, one-size-fits-all approaches aimed at mythical, generic "non-Christians" will not work. Such inflexible patterns appear as often in recently published books on culturally relevant ministry as they do in the calcified traditions of aging denominational congregations. Whatever our church situation, we desperately need to use *an array* of practices that can be implemented in response to a range of people.

It's easy to overlook the importance of developing a diversity of good practices. Until a few years ago, in fact, it wasn't particularly essential to do so. Church involvement was a part of most Western people's lives. Even if they did not attend regularly or even believe strongly, people did generally identify as members, and there were few other religious possibilities on the table. Being atheist or spiritual but not religious were not even deemed options by most of the population. If you wanted to become serious about the big questions of life, you simply found a decent church.

This all made evangelism pretty simple. Christians just needed to prioritize improvements to the church experience, such as making its message purer or more accessible, its community life more friendly or its music richer or livelier. Even today, much that is written about evangelism in the West assumes that the key to successfully engaging newcomers with Jesus is either the Sunday service or some spinoff, such as the small group structure.

But this focus on improving the core gatherings of the church, while still vitally important, is no longer sufficient. Martin Smith's discovery of Jesus, exemplary of so many similar contemporary spiritual journeys, was facilitated by a visit to a youth group, a friendship with a Christian, casual conversations over dinner with a family, the lyrics of a borrowed CD, arguments encountered in books, and occasional Sunday visits to a Pentecostal church. None of these, aside from the youth group visits, led to any regular, ongoing involvement in programmed church activities.

When I first met Martin, two weeks after his public response at the church service, he was only just beginning to consider committing to a local congregation. It's not that church hadn't previously been important. On the contrary, it had been vital. The church—meaning the members of "a covenant community centered around Jesus"—had been the ones through whom Christ had been made tangible, desirable and plausible to Martin.[7] But the role of Sundays, and indeed of *any* centrally programmed event, was only a tiny piece of Martin's journey.

Making Jesus tangible to most people outside the church, then, is going to mean remodeling more than just the Sunday services or the small group structure. We must also identify other practices that can help people to begin following Jesus for themselves.

WORSHIP AND EVANGELISM IN THE EARLY CHURCH

The early church certainly believed in the evangelistic power of whole-church gatherings. Paul vividly describes to the Corinthians his expectation that newcomers would be so struck by what they experience that they "will fall down and worship God, exclaiming, 'God is really among you!'" (1 Cor 14:25). It's the ancient equivalent of hoping that a Martin will walk forward at the end of a service to make a response. Yet, despite this intense belief in the potential of regular church meetings, Paul and his team never turned up in a town and simply launched a worship service. They always engaged in additional handpicked practices.

PICKING GOOD PRACTICES: FIRST CASE STUDY

The key to developing contextually appropriate, tangibility-establishing practices is simple to grasp, as evidenced by two of the most radically relevant churches I know.

One of them grew rapidly during its first two years of existence, in a busy port city marked by intense pagan spirituality. The local economy was partially dependent on the crowds of spiritual wanderers who would pass through and buy trinkets relating to an ancient female deity said to increase the fertility of her devotees. Her shrine, containing a carved meteorite, was famed all around the region. Many locals claimed to have obtained mystical powers upon visiting it, and the appearance of being able to work magic could lead to a lucrative income.[8]

Though the city was itself home to this very distinct spiritual environment, it was also part of a relatively intellectual wider culture where competing philosophies and ideas were constantly debated and subject to intense scrutiny, even by ordinary folks. A new idea could win interest quickly but would have to be convincing if it were to gather followers.

Into this environment of first-century Ephesus stepped Paul and his church-planting team. Paul, after three months of discussions with the Jews in the synagogue, turned his attention to the wider pagan population (Acts 19:8-9). He is recorded as engaging repeatedly in two specific practices that eventually made Jesus tangible to the whole city and beyond.

The first practice was public conversation. Paul based himself at a local lecture hall and had "discussions daily" there with all who would come. Paul knew that fresh philosophies attracted attention in Greek culture. So he leveraged this to his advantage by inviting people to interact in a typical philosophical setting with the novel message about Jesus. "In antiquity," writes biblical scholar Ben Witherington, "an orator or philosopher, in order to get a real hearing, needed to speak or teach in an appropriate place for such activities, whether it be in the home of a patron or in a public lecture hall."[9] By his own admission, Paul was not a great public speaker (2 Cor 10:10). But after two years of public discussions many of the locals were said to have "heard the word of the Lord" as a result of his efforts (Acts 19:10).

Paul also engaged in a public prayer and healing ministry. His Spirit-empowered works captured the imagination of the spiritually curious Ephesians, and they began treating him like a powerful

POWER AND PERSUASION

Paul is described as engaging in both reasoned debate *and* healing. It is rare in the West these days to see verbal apologetics and an emphasis on the contemporary miraculous power of God combined. But they can have a powerful impact when practiced together.

magician. They even used objects that had touched him to heal others (Acts 19:11-12).

Events in Ephesus culminated when some locals tried to mimic his exorcism style on a possessed man. They mistook Paul's usual formula of authoritative words about Jesus for a magic spell. It failed spectacularly and only provoked their demonized target into a violent attack. Suddenly it was vividly apparent that Paul's God-given power was of an entirely different category from magic. Soon a crowd of local former pagans voluntarily gathered to torch their valuable magical scrolls in the heat of a roaring bonfire as an act of turning to the Jesus they had all heard about from Paul in the lecture hall. Jesus had become so compelling that the value of what was being burned (more than 160 years' worth of wages) seemed negligible by comparison (Acts 19:13-19).[10]

The fire is an amazing scene made possible through Paul's persistent use of the practices of public prayer and discussion. The former made Jesus' authority vividly tangible, while the latter positioned Jesus as a plausible, and presumably also desirable, philosophical option. Together they made the reality, beauty and trustworthiness of Jesus unavoidable.

Note that Paul didn't do anything very original. The early church was quite accustomed to discussing with outsiders and praying for miracles. But because of the philosophical fixation of urban Greece and the specific spiritual environment within Ephesus, these two

---

BOOK BURNINGS?

Book burnings nowadays have grim historical associations with totalitarian regimes such as Nazism. It's worth emphasizing, then, that Paul doesn't command or suggest a book burning. The Ephesians do it spontaneously and voluntarily.

aspects of normal Christian practice—discussion and prayer—became the keys to reaching the entire city.

PICKING GOOD PRACTICES: SECOND CASE STUDY

The story of Ephesus is helpful as we think through how to make Jesus tangible in our own settings. We, like Paul, need to identify those basic aspects of following Jesus that are of particular value for our context. We must uncover those specific elements of *ordinary* Christian living that take on *extraordinary* importance among the people we are seeking to engage.

One British church I know has done this astonishingly well. Every Sunday it gathers a racially diverse group of people to praise God together. Many are immigrants who first came to the country as international students or asylum seekers. It's so successful at reaching multiple ethnicities that it's planted Chinese, French-speaking African and Arabic congregations over the years. The latter sees a steady stream of Muslims begin following Jesus.

Yet were you to walk into its Sunday gatherings, this same church seems like the very opposite of contextually aware. Most attendees wear suits, the entire service lacks any interaction beyond communal singing, ancient hymns are accompanied by an aging pipe organ, and the Bible readings are even taken from the King James Version. It is far from what most of us would conceive of as "relevant."

How, then, has it managed to successfully engage such a range of ethnicities? It has done so partly through a simple practice. Any newcomer who turns up on a Sunday, immigrant or not, will likely get invited for lunch at someone's house. This is no accident. The church discovered many decades ago that welcoming people into your home for food is almost the *only* way to form meaningful relationships with many non-Westerners. Acting on this knowledge has enabled them to make Christ tangible to a segment of the population with whom many churches fail to connect. Almost every non-Westerner who begins following Jesus through this church finds that their journey to so doing includes substantial time at the dinner tables of various church members.

The lesson here isn't that we should use relevance in one area as an excuse to neglect it in another. I would still suggest this church rethink their Sunday gatherings. Doing so might enable them to further increase the tangibility of how they present the Christian faith. Using contemporary language and more intelligible songs would likely help people like me, as well as immigrants with a shaky grasp on English, to better sense the immediacy and import of what is being said. But this church's example does highlight the textured nature of contextual sensitivity. We often want to reduce relevance and tangibility down to something like improving the music on a Sunday. Yet by making additional changes in our churches we can have even more impact and help open people to the reality of Jesus.

This church isn't doing anything very novel. Every follower of Jesus needs to be hospitable (1 Pet 4:9). When reaching out to non-Western newcomers, however, hospitality carries a vastly enlarged level of significance. Hospitality thus becomes the key that opens the door to Christianity in the same way that healing prayer and public discussion did in Ephesus, family life did for Martin and music did for Tamara.

Table 3.2

The Three Types of Practice Described in Each "Practices" Chapter		
	Useful for engaging:	Likely to be implemented by:
Micro Practices	one or two other people	you alone, or possibly with a friend
Meso Practices	small groups of people	you, perhaps with a friend or two
Macro Practices	large numbers of people	those with *any* level of leadership responsibility

The question, for those of us seeking to engage with a primarily Western-raised demographic, is, What practices might have the equivalent impact among our friends? What would help us when engaging with home-grown atheists, those who are spiritual but not religious and nominal Christians? Chapters six, nine and twelve provide a provisional answer to this question (see table 3.2).

BEING CATALYSTS

The process of making Jesus tangible, then, is one we can catalyze by identifying and emphasizing the most impactful practices for the group we are intending to reach. Perhaps it will entail something as simple as having more people over for dinner. After I told one of my friends who lives in Romania the story about the hospitable church, he went right out and bought a bigger kitchen table so he could more easily welcome people into his home.

Other times, though, it won't be quite so easy. Profound changes will be needed on an individual and community level. There is a beauty, though, to witnessing a Martin or Tamara shift from skepticism to seeking as they begin to realize that Christianity could actually be real.

C. S. Lewis compares such a transition to the moment "when the children who have been playing at burglars hush suddenly: was that a real footstep in the hall?"[11] The game becomes a reality, and everything changes. So it is with discovering God. Lewis comments that this can be as terrifying an experience as it is enlightening, adding:

> There comes a moment when people who have been dabbling in religion ("Man's search for God"!) suddenly draw back. Supposing we really found Him? We never meant it to come to that! Worse still, supposing He had found us?[12]

Yet without this moment or period of awakening to the tangible reality of Jesus, there can be no opportunity for anyone to accept or reject him. He will simply remain a plausible possibility or a desirable fantasy. Tangibility is therefore essential.

TAKING IT FURTHER

Whom would you like to see begin following Jesus? Picture that person in your mind right now and bring to mind all you know about them. Perhaps jot some thoughts here:

Now think about the Christians you know. Which one or two of them is most similar to this person you would like to see start following Jesus? Phone, email, text or message that Christian right now and arrange to meet up with them soon. When you get together, ask to hear the story of how they came to faith. As you listen, ask good questions and see whether you can identify what made Jesus tangible to them. Is it something that might also help your friend who does not yet know Jesus?

STORIES

The Temple in the Desert and the Mysterious Massage

The temple was a wooden pyramid surrounded by an expanse of gray sand as fine as flour. I locked my bicycle and approached it slowly and apprehensively, unaccustomed to entering such places.

As I entered the temple, a sea of bodies was all around me. Some were sleeping serenely, others were sobbing inconsolably, while many more wrote deep and heartfelt words on the wooden walls of this structure.

The smell of incense permeated the air, diffused from canisters waved by the temple guards. The words on the walls spoke of grief, of loss, and of desires unfulfilled.

"RIP Nephew, ur with my little bro now," read one scrawled message.

"I love you Catherine, but I have to let you go," said another beside it.

Another person simply wrote "forgive me," underneath which other hands had added the words "you're forgiven" and "it's not your fault."

At the center of the temple was an altar. Abstract and made from what looked like polished black rock, it was adorned with photographs and personal artifacts, such as glasses from deceased relatives, placed there by the people who had visited.

Less than forty-eight hours after my visit, the temple and all its contents would be burned to the ground in a ritual act. A crowd would watch and weep in silence as their innermost thoughts and outpourings were consumed by the flames.

Where was I?

India? Africa?

No . . . I was in the United States of America.

This was the temple at Burning Man, an annual festival in the Nevada desert attended by tens of thousands of (mainly) wealthy white Westerners. Burning Man is a place where the often-hidden spiritual hunger of Western people blows its own cover for a few days each year and is made visible for all to see. Burning Man began as a festival of self-expression in 1980s San Francisco but later migrated to the desert. A sprawling temporary city, complete with enormous, interactive works of art and a roaming fleet of neon "mutant cars," is now erected every August and becomes the site of both wild hedonism and also sincere spiritual seeking.

Despite my own misgivings as I entered the temple, there was such a rawness of emotion on display among participants that I soon found myself sitting and weeping with one of them, who showed me a painfully honest four-page letter she had written about her need to experience deep change and transformation. She pleaded (to whom, it was not clear) for freedom from a cycle of using her own sexuality to boost her self-esteem. She repeatedly begged forgiveness for all she had done to others over the past year. It ached me just to read it.

Later, I walked past another temple-goer whose tear-soaked face was a picture of desolation. I felt drawn to offer him a hug, and we stood there together for several silent minutes as he clung to me and his warm tears soaked into the shoulder of my T-shirt. As we parted, he thanked me sincerely and moved on to write a poem to a former lover on a nearby wooden beam.

When I eventually left the temple, I noticed a striking contrast between those leaving and those arriving. Whereas the newcomers walked slowly, but with essentially the same manner one might adopt when first entering an unfamiliar pub, those leaving seemed serene, and their thoughts appeared to be fixed on something other than themselves or their surroundings.

Anyone who spends time walking slowly through the Burning Man temple can no longer believe the unchurched in the West have all moved on from a desire for deep spiritual experience, for healing, for forgiveness, for ritual and even for religion.

THE TENT

The temple was far from the only place of spiritual expression and encounter at Burning Man. Two days earlier I'd found myself sitting on one of the comfortable cushions in a small circular tent quilted together from a range of vibrantly colored fabrics. The tent was wide enough for me to lie down in but too low to stand up. I'd been drawn there because I was seeking a place of quiet where I could escape the crowds and just sit in relative silence. I had no idea about its spiritual dimension until I'd entered.

I discovered that the tent contained only the cushions, some books and a table covered by an eclectic assortment of objects. These items included a wax skull, a stone Buddha, several candles, some beautiful seashells, several smooth stones and vibrant crystals, a bunch of in-cense sticks, some beautiful tiny metal boxes, and a lighter for the candles and incense. I looked at the table for a while and wondered who had put it together and why they had done so.

I then picked up one of the books and began reading. Their pages contained the intimate, handwritten thoughts of various anonymous individuals who had attended Burning Man over the past few years.

One person wrote that they had experienced a mystical sense of rediscovering self there in the desert. The author mused that "we all long for place. And place itself longs [for us]." Just being at Burning Man, this person said, made him or her feel as though "a thousand birds flew out of my heart."

Another hand penned the words, "I come to the same revelation every year here. It's not about me. It's about us."

Though reading these books lacked the emotional intensity of the temple, I found it compelling to read these strangers' experiences through the felt-tip words they had left behind. The Alone Dome, as this tent was called, was born from the imagination of Kate, a young nutritionist from San Francisco. I first met Kate just as I had finished reading the books. As we sat together under the dome, barely big enough to hold two people, I asked her why she had created this space.

Kate replied that she often felt overwhelmed by the crowds of people at Burning Man and needed a place to recalibrate herself. This led her to create "a space where people felt like they could be who they are and do what they needed to do." Prayer, meditation and simply resting were three of the things she said happened in the Alone Dome. The books and the table were there to provide a focal point for these activities.

As the conversation continued, I asked Kate about her own spiritual journey. She told me that she had never been a part of any organized religion and her upbringing was entirely secular. But throughout her childhood she had become increasingly aware of something good and beautiful beyond the physical. This awareness sometimes found expression in art or dance but was always hovering in the background.

When she went to college, Kate connected with a group of people who would spend long hours having deep discussions about life. It was the first time she had been part of a community that was willing to talk at length about big questions of existence and meaning. Kate also took classes where she learned to dismantle assumed ideas and interpretations of culture. This confirmed her previous intuition that there were more possible ways of understanding reality than those she had been presented with thus far. Perhaps, as she had thought for so many years, she really was surrounded by a spiritual reality.

There was no dramatic turning point for Kate, but the years since college had been an ongoing process of "opening up to an ever-present spirit of love, or of goodness, and opening [my] heart to this power that's waiting for us, that's all around us." She said she sometimes calls this spirit "God," and it was a source of "very big acceptance and gratitude. . . . It's not like I'm seeing beauty and feeling a love based on what I see. It's just that suddenly it's there."

Kate, an intelligent woman from a nonreligious background, had meandered her way into encountering an unknown and apparently loving spiritual reality. So profoundly important is her experience that she creates and hauls a tent into the desert every year so that strangers can come and have quiet spiritual moments of their own. It's a striking story. It is not, however, a unique one.

THE HIDDEN TRIBE

Kate is one among many people who would call themselves spiritual but not religious. Most people with whom I spoke at Burning Man used some variation of this phrase to describe themselves.

It's a slippery term that often seems to indicate both a sense of connection with some unseen reality and a lack of identification with any organized religious grouping or doctrinal framework. That unseen or "spiritual" dimension of reality is variously described as a state of mind, an angel, a god or very frequently just as a force or energy.

Other times, as we'll see in the next chapter, *spirituality* simply means treating people and the world as special and sacred. For the rest of this chapter, though, we'll focus on the first sense of the term; an intuition that it might be possible to connect with "the non-material animating principle of life," whether that is defined as "God" or something else altogether.[1]

The existence of the spiritual but not religious has crept under the radar of both the Christian church and also the wider media. Many of us are accustomed to mentally categorizing those outside the Christian faith in one of the following categories:

- Muslim
- Jewish

- Hindu
- Buddhist
- atheist
- agnostic

If someone is not a Christian or a member of another religion we assign them to the last two groups on the list, atheist or agnostic. Many atheists implicitly accept the same categorization system. One self-professed atheist comments that:

> Atheism is the default state of all human beings. It takes no action on the part of the person to be Atheist. Atheist is what we would all be if there were no vile old men molding children's minds to suit their agenda, or moronic parents inflicting their own stupidity on their children.[2]

At first glance, these words seem to contain nothing a Christian might affirm. For the most part, this impression is true. But the

---

SPIRITUALITY IS INBUILT

Justin Barrett, cognitive scientist at Oxford University and Fuller Seminary, notes how extensive research among children shows them to have an inbuilt "cognitive bias to see the natural world as purposefully designed by non-human agency."[3] "For instance," he says, "children are inclined to say rocks are 'pointy' not because of some physical processes but because being pointy keeps them from being sat upon. . . . Research suggests that even 12-month-olds understand that only intentional beings create order from disorder."[4] We are, he concludes, literally "born believers" for whom "acquiring the notion of [God] . . . presents no special difficulties."[5]

writer does express an ordinarily unspoken assumption shared by many Christians: namely, if a Western person is not part of a major religion, then he or she is probably an atheist or materialist with no consciously spiritual dimension to their understanding and experience of the world. Christians and atheists, then, are unwittingly collaborating to perpetuate the myth that a person who eschews conventional religion defaults to a life free from prayer, ritual or transcendent experience.

Nothing, however, could be further from the truth. Atheists remain a minority in global terms, with the highest estimates suggesting that just 13 percent of the world population are atheists.[6] The highest concentrations are in Japan and China. The latter of these two nations is in the midst of an ongoing Christian revival that has seen tens of millions begin following Jesus over the past three decades. In the United States figures for atheism remain low; the highest estimates still hover around 7 percent, as discussed in chapter one. If anything, it seems like the *default* direction is toward the opposite of atheism. As the late atheist and fantasy novelist Terry Pratchett writes: "Whoever had created humanity had left in a major design flaw. It was its tendency to bend at the knees."[7] This reflex to kneel before something—or someone—bigger than ourselves remains irresistible for the majority of the world's population.

"SPIRITUAL" VERSUS "NEW AGE"

The spiritual but not religious have not entirely escaped the attention of Jesus' followers. We Christians have attempted over recent decades to find space for them on our demographic maps. The label "New Age" is often used by authors and speakers as an umbrella term for the beliefs and practices of such individuals.

New Age, however, is an unhelpful term for describing people like Kate or the crowds in the temple. It partly fails because the spiritual but not religious are too diverse to be categorized using so concrete a label. They include pantheists who believe in an all-pervasive Star

Wars kind of force, polytheists who think there are a range of spiritual beings with whom we can interact, monotheists who believe in a single supremely creative entity, and even atheists.

One person I interviewed at Burning Man told me that he had grown up Quaker but now "believes in science" and completely dismisses the possible existence of God. He then went to explain how he was also open to the possibility of angels and even thinks they may be involved in his life. He laughed at his own inconsistency even as he told me this. I laughed too: when you meet an atheist who thinks he may be visited by angels, it reminds you that many people's spirituality is too complex and patchwork to be neatly slotted into any existing category such as New Age.

New Age itself is a highly elastic category, but a strict interpretation of the term would include a sense that humanity is evolving into a new era (or "age") in which states of altered consciousness (attained through drugs, meditation or other means) allow us to access the unseen reality around us and thereby enable us to transcend space, time and even our own mortality.[8] It grew out of the 1960s hippie movement and represents a very narrow segment of those who describe themselves as spiritual but not religious.

Even for people who really can accurately be categorized as New Age, it is usually a viewpoint into which they have drifted unaware. Their very addendum of "and not religious" suggests that they genuinely see themselves as standing outside any recognizable philosophical framework or movement. It is unlikely to aid our interactions with them, therefore, if we use an understanding of New Age as *the* key to engaging with their perspective or experience.

Not all those who are spiritual but not religious, then, are like Kate from the Alone Dome, and not all express this dimension of themselves in places like the Burning Man temple. The experiences of those who are spiritual but not religious cover a wide range of views. This group needs to be understood as distinct from (though sometimes overlapping with) New Age or atheist.

TOWARD OR AWAY?

I was recently at a party when a friend said something that encapsulated the way Christians frequently view people who are spiritual but not religious. We were chatting over drinks and he said, "I admire you for going into a place where people are so opposed to the Christian faith." He went on to tell me how wonderful he thought it was that I was going to Burning Man and engaging with people who were estranged from the church by bad experiences or negative encounters with professed believers.

What struck me about his otherwise lovely and encouraging words was that they contained an unchecked assumption I once shared. I also used to think that anybody in the West pursuing a "nonreligious" spirituality was likely to take a dim view of Christianity and probably had some past experiences that had caused disillusionment with the church.

My understanding could be visualized like this:

| Openness to Christianity | Negative church experience or impression | Embrace of other spiritualities |

Figure 4.1

People who would otherwise default to Christianity, I assumed, had now been driven into the arms of other spiritual beliefs and experiences. But as I began to encounter more people who are spiritual but not religious, I found that few of them even had any firsthand experience of the church. Not many have strong views about Christianity, some even have purely positive impressions of Christians, and most are well-disposed toward (though ill-informed about) Jesus.[9]

I recently shared these discoveries with another Christian friend of mine and told him I didn't think it was true that people were being pulled *away* from Christianity through their experience of other spiritualities. My friend replied that I might be right, but surely such spiritualities cannot be pushing people *toward* the Christian faith. I responded by telling him the story of Anna, a computer programmer from Wyoming.

Anna grew up in an entirely nonreligious family. She'd never taken much notice of religion and, like her parents, was an agnostic who was uninterested in spirituality. This remained the case until her late thirties when her boyfriend's mother, a masseuse, offered her a free massage. While she was on the table, having her muscles pressed, she suddenly found herself, in her own words, "transported out of her body and into some kind of entirely alternate reality." She remained there for several minutes before returning to her own body. The whole thing was completely unexpected. Her previous worldview was shattered. It was all so vividly real that she is now convinced that there is more to reality than we can see or measure. She is open to learning and developing spiritually (we had a good conversation together about Jesus), but nobody is guiding or helping her to do so.

The contours of Anna's story are similar to those of Kate, with whom I chatted at the Alone Dome. Both cases feature a person who grew up in an entirely nonreligious, secular environment, had some kind of experience that opened them to connecting with some unseen reality (whether a dramatic massage or the slow influence of friends and professors) and who is now open to further discovery and redefinition of exactly who or what is behind their experiences.

If one were to depict Anna's and Kate's spiritual journeys, it might look similar to this:

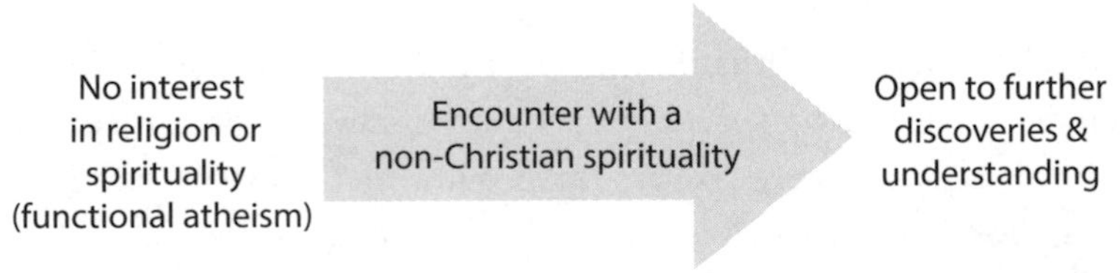

No interest in religion or spirituality (functional atheism) → Encounter with a non-Christian spirituality → Open to further discoveries & understanding

Figure 4.2

Non-Christian spiritual experience, then, does not necessarily lead people away from Jesus. It may in fact ease them out of their cozy assumptions about the world and open them up to the possibility that something out there (perhaps even God) is real and is personally interested in connecting with them. We might say that the tangibility of *all* spiritualities, including Christian ones, are enhanced when a person has *any* such experiences.

THE MESSINESS OF SPIRITUALITY

Not everything in the world of those who are spiritual but not religious is positive and helpful. The visit to the Burning Man temple was perhaps the most unsettling thing to happen to me in years, and I barely slept for a week afterwards. Part of what troubled me was that I had encountered a warm and inviting presence in the temple. It was something neither emotional nor psychological. I knew I was experiencing something genuinely spiritual, as real as any past encounter with God, and that it wanted me to come close and open myself to it.

It reminded me of contemporary artist Ray Caesar, who said that he began creating his work as a child when he was visited by a mysterious woman. She would appear in the corner of his room and tell soft stories to him in periods of personal distress. Soon thereafter an anonymous intelligence would take over his body and control his hand, causing him to draw things of which his mind had never conceived. He says that he has "always felt the presence of a kindly 'Other' that is both 'part and separate' of my own entity" and it has been a major catalyst in his own artistic development.[10]

It seems, then, that encounters with spirits are not always unsettling and they can sometimes feel friendly and welcoming. But this does not mean such experiences are good or that they are always manifestations of God. A few days after I had finally managed to sleep again following my time in the temple, I was speaking at a conference in Romania and started chatting with a friend who is preparing to be a missionary in India. He told me that the previous week he had been in Delhi and had viewed some video footage of an Indian pastor and a man on the street who seemed in great distress. The minister sensed there was something demonic at play, so he turned to the troubled individual and commanded that the demon leave him. The distressed man's voice and face suddenly changed beyond recognition as the demon refused to come out. The pastor said, "I cast you out to hell," and the demon began begging and pleading that it be allowed to return to the nearby temple from which it came. The pastor refused its request and again commanded the demon leave and be damned. The man shook and writhed, then finally a peace came over him as whatever had previously afflicted him left. It was as though he had become human again.

Among all the dramatic elements of my friend's tale, one detail stood out: the demon wanted to *return* to the temple. This was its home, and where it presumably first latched onto its poor victim.

I should emphasize that not all temples are homes of demons, and not all other religious expressions are as dark as the one encountered by my friend. Neither are the spiritual but not religious ordinarily "possessed" or demonized. The overwhelming majority are certainly not. But we must be cautious in assuming that all that is "spiritual" is beneficial, or that every unseen reality experienced by others is a positive development. Some spiritual experiences may be catalysts toward God, but others may draw people in the opposite direction.

EARLY CHRISTIAN RESPONSES

Twice in the book of Acts, we find extended accounts of the apostle Paul interacting with people who are pagan and not Jewish. In some ways these are the closest first-century equivalents of people who are spiritual but not religious. Paul seems to take quite different approaches on each occasion.

The first time Paul is hailed as a god after being used to heal a lame man (Acts 14:8-20). People actually rush to offer sacrifices to him. They even decide that his traveling partner, Barnabas, is the living embodiment of Zeus. A crowd gathers, and Paul directly confronts it. He calls them to stop worshiping people or idols. Their gods, he says, are "worthless things," and they should turn immediately "to the living God." He draws a very clear dividing line between reaching for their gods and experiencing the one true God. They must, he insists, choose one and reject the other.

A few chapters later we find Paul giving a speech to a group of powerful, philosophically minded individuals (Acts 17:16-34). He strikes up conversation with some of them after seeing all the idols in their city. These interactions lead to a speaking invitation for Paul, and he begins his talk by describing one of the local idols he saw. Unlike other similar statues, he notes, it bears the enigmatic title "To an Unknown God." Paul then says, "you are ignorant of the very thing you worship—and this is what I am going to proclaim to you." Note that this time he doesn't tell people to stop worshiping their god but instead says, "You are ignorant of the very thing you worship—and this is what I am going to proclaim to you." There is still a strong element of challenge to Paul's message as he exhorts listeners to "leave their existing conceptions of the divine" (paraphrase mine), but he also treats their current spiritual lives as something that can be built upon, rather than something that must be entirely rejected.

It seems, then, that there is sufficient biblical warrant for Christians to address other spiritualities in a range of ways. We do sometimes need to follow Paul's first example of highlighting contrasts between people's current spiritual experience and the reality of knowing "the living God."

But this approach isn't the only one available. When talking to someone like Kate, for example, we don't necessarily have to call her away from her current experience of "an ever-present spirit of love . . . of goodness . . . that's waiting for us, that's all around us."

We can instead agree with her that there *is* someone who is loving, good and all around us. Then we can share how Jesus (along with the wider scriptural portrait of God) sketches in the details of this someone.

We therefore need to keep an open mind when it comes to engaging with the spiritual but not religious. Their experiences may be veiled encounters with God himself, or they may be something altogether less healthy. We can only really know as we listen to them share their stories with us.

CLOSER TO HOME

As you read this chapter, did anybody you know spring to mind? Are there people in your world whom you would describe as spiritual but not religious?

I wondered, after I left the temple, what these people do when they are not weeping and meditating at Burning Man. I tried to imagine some of them in their places of work, local neighborhoods or college lectures. Did anybody around them actually know about the depth of their spiritual longing or the profundity of their ritualized experiences in the desert? Almost nobody I spoke with at Burning Man was part of any ongoing community or group where they discussed or experienced such things. Perhaps it all remains hidden under the surface.

So even if you think you know no one who is spiritual but not religious, you actually do; it's just that they have simply never revealed that aspect of themselves to you. It may be something so private that it has never been shared with anyone, not even at a remote location like a temple in the Nevada desert.

People who are spiritual but not religious don't spend the majority of their time in temples or meditation tents. Most never visit such places. Even if they do, most of their days are still spent living and working near you. Maybe they would just love an opportunity to share the spiritual side of themselves with somebody like you.

TAKING IT FURTHER

If you are not sure whether your nonreligious friend has a spiritual dimension to their life, a great way to gently raise the issue is to ask a simple question.

A good question is one that allows you to listen to (and interact with) the other person's story. So, find a time when you can be uninterrupted for a few minutes, perhaps during a lunch break or over coffee, and ask one of the following questions:

"I'm just curious, would you describe yourself as a spiritual person?"

After they respond, ask them "why?" or "why not?" Then listen and let the conversation flow.

"I was wondering: Do you ever pray?"

You can follow up with questions such as "Have you always prayed?" "What do you pray about?" or "To whom or what are you praying?" Again, it's vital to focus on listening and letting the conversation unfold naturally. These kinds of questions, if asked in a spirit of genuine inquiry and with an authentic desire to listen, can help create a safe space for our friends who are spiritual but not religious to share this side of themselves.

QUESTIONS

Does Christianity Enable a Richer Spirituality?

Spirituality is a form of thirst. People who call themselves spiritual usually attempt, or at least aspire, to live a more satisfying existence than they currently enjoy. They do not follow Jesus because they have not realized, or have maybe even consciously rejected, the possibility that he could satiate their craving.

THIRSTY WIZARDS

Ursula Le Guin, an author who weaves questions of spirituality throughout her popular fantasy novels, tells a story that encapsulates the experience of many who are spiritual but not religious. It is about two trainee wizards who go for a walk. As they climb a hill together, Jasper, the more experienced of the pair, begins needling newcomer Ged to show him some kind of illusion or spell.

Ged resists Jasper. He doesn't want to use his sorcery for showmanship and self-validation. Instead he asks Jasper to demonstrate his own skills. Jasper accepts the challenge:

> Pointing his finger Jasper spoke a few strange words, and where he pointed on the hillside among the green grasses a little thread

of water trickled, and grew, and now a spring gushed out and the water went running down the hill. Ged put his hand in the stream and it felt wet, drank of it and it was cool. Yet for all that it would quench no thirst, being an illusion. Jasper with another word stopped the water and the grasses waved dry in the sunlight.[1]

Ged is unimpressed. This is not the kind of magic he desires. Jasper's "games of seeming" only affect the appearance of things and fail completely to produce something real or satisfying.[2]

A "spiritual" person who says they are "not religious" is often claiming to be Ged to the religious person's Jasper. They see religious institutions, doctrines and practices as offering little more than illusionary, unsatisfying water. Far better, they conclude, to reach for something real and capable of quenching their thirst for a fuller existence.

They tend to pursue this satisfying spiritual reality in two different directions: "upwards" and "outwards," according to author Linda Mercadante, whose book *Belief Without Borders* is the most thorough piece of recent research into the beliefs of the spiritual but not religious.[3] She describes upwards and outwards spirituality in these ways:

Upwards Spirituality	Outwards Spirituality
A stretching of the self "towards God, Higher Power, the cosmos, the 'Ultimate,' or some other . . . reality beyond the material world."	A desire to live a life that moves "beyond one's limited ego, out to others, the world, community, nature, and so on."

Figure 5.1. Source: Linda Mercadante, *Belief Without Borders* (Oxford: Oxford University Press, 2014), 94.

Upwards spirituality, in short, reaches for something beyond the human and physical, the kind of spirituality that I emphasized in the previous chapter. Outwards spirituality is more focused on our world and the people in it, as I will discuss in this chapter.

As we converse with people who are spiritual but not religious, we should bear these two categories in mind. Some people primarily (or even solely) define their spirituality in outwards terms. They have little interest in experiencing God or connecting with the immaterial reality that sustains life. Others are more upwards focused and have limited concern for embracing the wider world. Still others have a spirituality that combines both outwards and upwards dimensions. The questions and concerns we encounter will vary according to the weight our conversation partners place on each aspect of spirituality.

Those who are spiritual but not religious will have their own blend of reasons for not embracing Christianity. You'll need to identify these as you talk with them as they probably won't use the terms *upwards* and *outwards*. There are, however, two key themes that recur frequently:

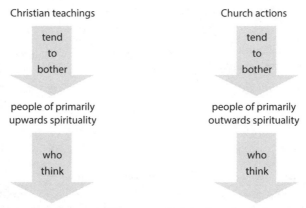

Christian teachings	Church actions
tend to bother	tend to bother
people of primarily upwards spirituality	people of primarily outwards spirituality
who think	who think
"Why have doctrinal frameworks? The rigid beliefs of most major world religions are a threat to the vitality and freedom of my personal quest for the transcendent."	*"Religion has advanced so many terrible causes, from the crusades through to child abuse scandals and homophobia. It is incompatible with spiritual health."*

Figure 5.2

Teachings and actions. It's not an exhaustive list, but a high proportion of questions from people who are spiritual but not religious relate to one of these two categories. Note that the accent of both is on the desirability of the Christian faith rather than its plausibility. In comparison to atheism, Christianity does not elicit as many debates about the factuality and intellectual tenability of its basic beliefs. People will likely assume Christianity's plausibility if its desirability and tangibility are apparent.[4]

A third theme that people commonly express is an opposition to organized or institutional religion. What is interesting about this objection is that in my experience people rarely object to the idea that spiritually minded people should somehow structure their lives together or build communities. So if you ask a person why they don't like organized religion they will likely cite Christian teachings, church actions or bad experiences of a local congregation. Questions about institutional religion, in other words, usually turn out to be about something else other than organizations or institutionalism. For this reason I would suggest that you respond to anyone with this objection by asking why they hold this viewpoint. You'll likely discover that their real concerns lie elsewhere.

REIMAGINING CHURCH

Church takes a range of forms. There's a big movement among Christians in the West today to reimagine what church should look like in our current rapidly shifting culture.[5] When a person questions the value of church or religion as they have experienced it until now, then, they are joining in a conversation already occurring among Jesus' followers. Rather than defend religion, then, perhaps we should inquire about their experience (or perception) of it. We can also ask people what they think an intentional community inspired by Jesus and his teachings would look like in our current context. Spark their imagination about the potential of church rather than allowing their past experiences to limit the possibilities.

So the next question is how we can conversationally engage questions about church actions and Christian teachings. How do we avoid looking like conjurers of imaginary water to our spiritually thirsty friends?

CHURCH ACTIONS AND OUTWARDS SPIRITUALITY

Let's start with misgivings about the church's actions. Many of those with an outwards-focused spirituality question whether Christianity has any potential to enrich the world.

Those who are spiritual but not religious may not be able to articulate exactly what bothers them about the church's behavior. But if you speak with them for a while you will normally find that their concerns fall into one (or more) of four categories:

Table 5.1

	Scriptural Issues	Historical Issues	Contemporary Issues	Personal Experiences
Description	aspects of the Bible that seem to legitimize distasteful behavior	things the church has done in the past that suggest it is a force for bad, not good	what the church and Christians are up to at this exact moment in time, or very recently	things that have happened to them (or those they know) or they have witnessed firsthand
Examples	Old Testament genocides	the Crusades, slavery	homophobia, political alliances	abuse, unkindness, condemnation
Accompanying Emotions	usually mild	usually mild	varied	usually strong

When we encounter any of these criticisms, we may be tempted to immediately leap to the defense of the church. This response, though, would be a mistake. Many misgivings about the quality of Christians' outwards spirituality have some basis in reality. The Crusades, homophobia, tacit complicity in the slave trade and many other gruesome skeletons hang in the closet of the Christian church. Our best first step, then, is to simply acknowledge the very real failings of Christians and apologize.

I frequently find myself saying something like, "Sorry, the church has been a bit rubbish at times, hasn't it?" It's my honest opinion; we've frequently messed up. I'm not just saying it for effect. But you'd be surprised how much hostility to Christianity can be removed by simply admitting that we get it wrong much of the time.

We should be thoughtful, though, about *how* we apologize. Each category of question, as the above diagram shows, tends to have a different level of emotion attached to it. Simple acknowledgment of fault and apology may be sufficient in the case of most historical and some contemporary church failings. But our empathy and sense of sorrow must increase the more a person *feels* the gravity and pain of a specific instance of Christians failing and the more personal the issue is.

We may not be individually responsible for the offense in question, but we are representatives of the same church that perpetrated it. A person's sense of hurt toward injustice is often intensified by their feeling that "nobody ever apologized or admitted fault." We can be part of their healing by listening to their stories and being the face of Christ's sorrow over what happened.

One of my friends, Freda, says that apologies on the behalf of others can be tremendously healing. She was sexually assaulted by a stranger on a family vacation to Cyprus, which affected her profoundly as she struggled with anger toward the perpetrator mingled with an unjustified sense of personal shame. She felt that somehow she must have deserved what happened to her, and so she kept the experience to herself. As time went on her sense of suspicion toward men grew. She struggled to trust the males in her life and assumed that they were all secretly involved in some horrible sexual practices behind closed doors.

One evening at church, after years of living in oppression with these feelings, she heard a talk on healing at her local church. The visiting speaker said:

> There might be some of you out there who have been sexually violated. I am sorry. I am saying sorry because I am also a man. I know the high expectation that God has of us and how we should treat women, and I am sorry that some man failed to treat you with the love, value, worth and respect that you deserve.

You are precious, because you were created in God's image. You deserve to be treated in a way that reflects your value, and I'm sorry that somebody failed you and God. I'm sorry how it made you feel, how it affected your life.

Freda felt a sense of release in this moment. Somebody was taking the gravity of experiences like hers seriously and had apologized. Suspicion and shame began to loosen their grip on her. Freda began to pursue counseling and experienced healing over the months and years that followed. Later she met Ian, her husband, and they now enjoy a healthy marriage. But it was the speaker's apology that opened the door for Freda to transition from suspicion to trusting men again.

In the same way that the speaker owning the actions of his whole gender helped facilitate Freda's change in her relationships with men, Christians expressing genuine sorrow for the behavior of their brothers and sisters can do the same. The outcome may not be so cathartically dramatic for everyone we meet. Even for Freda it was just the start of a process. But at least we can show we care and open people's minds to the possibility that their past experience of church (and of Christians) may not be representative of the whole.

APOLOGIZING FOR SCRIPTURE?

Apology, though, is not the only thing we should offer. In fact, in the case of objections to Scripture, we need to be cautious of expressing regret. In my experience, when someone tells me the Bible condones something horrible, often they have misunderstood the text or been provided with faulty information.

This became very clear to me when I was speaking recently at a café-style event in the north of Romania. Iași is a beautiful city. But it is also the site of one of the worst pogroms in Jewish history; more than thirteen thousand Jews were publicly murdered in the street during one day in 1941, a fact I shared during my presentation.

A physiotherapy student named Oana approached me afterwards to thank me for my talk. She said it was her first time attending a Christian event. She considers herself a spiritual person, and what I said had resonated with her. Becoming a Christian, though, was completely off the table for her. She had read online about how the Old Testament, supposedly part of God's book, is full of violence and rape and murder. Her own brief perusal of its pages had confirmed that this was the case.

I agreed that bloodshed and misogyny are rife throughout the Old Testament, and that many of the scenes within are horrific. Then I added, smiling and intentionally being a little provocative, "And that's why I love it!"

Oana stared at me.

"That's why you love it?!" she said, intrigued and thankfully a little amused. "How can you love that kind of thing?"

"Well," I said, "Have you ever seen *Schindler's List*?"

"Oh yes, great movie, but very sad."

"Yes," I agreed, "it's brilliant. But it's also full of genocide, abuse, murder and rape. Is it an immoral movie?"

Oana replied immediately, "No, it's probably one of the most moral films ever made. It's taught millions of people about the horrors of the Holocaust."

"Exactly," I said. "It needed to portray those terrible things in order to tell an accurate story about that period of history. A Holocaust movie that only showed hugs, rainbows and fluffy bunnies would do no justice to the reality of what occurred."

"It would be ridiculous," she agreed.

"Right, and if the Bible is to be a book which tells us the truth about the dark realities of our world, as well as its beautiful aspects, it's going to have some pretty gruesome scenes. Almost half the Bible is straight narrative. But it's no more condoning all the terrible events it records than Steven Spielberg, the director of *Schindler's List*, was endorsing the Holocaust."

Oana thought for a moment and then replied, "So that's why you love that the Bible has these awful things in it. Not because those things are in themselves good?"

I agreed. "Any spirituality which makes a difference in the real world is going to have to be one that faces the nastiest aspects of reality square in the face. I think the Bible does that."

As she thought about this for a moment, I added, "I'll admit, there are a handful of tricky passages that give the impression that the Bible is not just recording events, but that God himself commissions some outrageous violence. But if you read them carefully, you'll find they're not all they seem. If you want to discuss those passages we could. But I'd be curious to know a little about your take on Jesus, because I think his story is the portion of the Bible that has most helped *me* understand not just that the world is dark, but that there is also hope in it."

TRICKY OLD TESTAMENT PASSAGES

You can read what I would have said to Oana on this topic in appendix two.

She wasn't too interested in detailed discussion of Old Testament passages. Relatively few people are. So we spoke instead for a while about Jesus. She had an intuition that he was a positive figure but knew little else about him.

I'd shared in my earlier talk that Jesus touched those with infectious, deforming skin diseases, was kind and welcoming (yet never physically involved) with sex workers, and yet for all his edgy, risk-taking actions, kids still felt comfortable casually approaching him, and he was constantly invited to parties. He displayed an unusual combination of passionately confronting the darkness and also being warmly approachable. As we talked Oana said that she'd found this a really attractive model of a spiritual life.

I asked her whether it was the kind of life she aspired to live.

"Definitely," she replied firmly.

I pulled out my phone and showed her a photo of my five-year-old son, Jackson, and his best friend making faces with their tongues sticking out. I told Oana that Jackson had first adopted a silly expression. Then his friend Eliana had copied him. I said, "I think that we are like Jackson and Eliana; we become like the people we spend time with."

Oana agreed. So I added, "And Jesus would often say to people 'come and follow me'; it was an invitation to spend time with him. It's in relationship with him, and not simply through a bit of knowledge about him, that we begin to emulate his example."

We spoke for a while about what it means to follow Jesus. But I could see that time was slipping away. So I suggested that one way to begin at least investigating Jesus would be to spend more time among people who are already committed to following him. Oana said she had enjoyed this event, so I took her contact information and told her we'd shoot her a message when we next had something going on.

The nasty aspects of the Bible, then, are not something for which we need to be ashamed. They show us that the Scriptures are realistic about the horrors of our world. The turbulent pages of the Old Testament raise the question of hope and transformation: as soon as we realize we're in darkness we begin searching for the light switch. My conversation with Oana therefore inevitably led to discussing Jesus.

My specific emphasis on Jesus' capacity to reshape us personally was intentional. In the days preceding my encounter with Oana, I had been reflecting on a passage written by Aleksandr Solzhenitsyn, a Russian dissident who spent years in Soviet prison camps:

> If only there were evil people somewhere insidiously committing evil deeds, and it were necessary only to separate them from the rest of us and destroy them. But the line dividing good and evil cuts through the heart of every human being. And who is willing to destroy a piece of his own heart?[6]

It is the human heart that is the root issue. Oana, like many people who are spiritual but not religious, aspires to live a good life. But the biggest hindrance to any of us fulfilling our high ideals is ourselves. Sharing our experiences of Jesus, along with explaining what it means to follow him, can open others' imaginations to the possibility that life with him could be the very thing to which their desires are pointing. We need, for sure, to clarify and address misunderstandings. But no hope can be offered, nor can any issue with Scripture be adequately dealt with, unless we eventually find ourselves discussing Jesus.

CLARIFYING THE CHURCH'S HISTORICAL AND CONTEMPORARY TRACK RECORD

Church history can be as easily misunderstood by our friends as can Scripture. Alongside our apologies for and acknowledgment of Christians' failings, then, we may sometimes need to clarify common misunderstandings about the church's role in history. Most of the time people are so chronologically distant, and therefore emotionally removed, from the events they mention that a simple response such as, "That was terrible, wasn't it?" will often suffice.

It's usually helpful to then add something such as, "But that's really not representative of the church's impact throughout history." One of the things I love about the Christian movement is that despite its frequent failures, it has an incredible track record for shaping the world positively. There are numerous concrete examples of how Jesus has inspired social change and how his followers have enacted it over the centuries. Our suggestion that following Jesus can make a difference in the world will lack credibility to an individual whose entire mental image of church history consists of the worst excesses. It will sound like a nice dream that has no basis in reality.

It can therefore help to cite an example or tell a story about a historical Christian who made a difference. There are many to choose from: William Wilberforce, an evangelical Christian, was the driving force behind the abolition of slavery in the Western world. Dietrich Bonhoeffer, a Lutheran pastor, was a key figure in the resistance against the Nazis in the 1930s. Emmeline Pankhurst, a passionate twentieth-century Christian, led the suffragette movement, which secured voting rights for women in Britain and Canada. The list goes on and on.

The three people I most frequently quote to others are Martin Luther King, Charles Malik and Toyohiko Kagawa. Each of them explicitly based their philosophy and practice on the teachings of Jesus. Here's more information about each one:

Table 5.2

	Martin Luther King	Charles Malik	Toyohiko Kagawa
Nationality	American	Lebanese	Japanese
Role	minister and activist	theologian and philosopher	writer and sociologist
Claim to Fame	led the civil rights movement; helped end segregation	coauthor of the UN Declaration of Human Rights	put an end to then-common practice of adoptive parents murdering their children
Key Quote	"Jesus Christ was an extremist for love, truth and goodness."	"The greatest thing about any civilization is the human person, and the greatest thing about this person is the possibility of his encounter with the person of Jesus Christ."	"In the heart of the God of the universe, each child of his is as necessary to him as the fingers are to the hand."

For other similar examples, spend time googling Oscar Romero, Thomas Barnardo, Paul Brand, Desmond Tutu or Lord Shaftsbury. They didn't just happen to be Christians. Each one was inspired by their faith in Jesus to take costly risks in order to help the poor and vulnerable.

Alongside these historical examples we can cite the many modern movements inspired by the teachings and example of Jesus. These include World Vision, one of the biggest humanitarian aid and development organizations operating today, and some of the most prominent current campaigns against human trafficking, such as Stop the Traffik and Not for Sale. All of these are explicitly rooted in Christian principles and draw much of their support and voluntary personnel from churches. They're just part of a much longer list. Here are a few other such well-known, Christian-based organizations:

- **International Justice Mission**: Rescues victims of human rights abuses

- **Compassion International**: Facilitates sponsorship of developing-world children

- **Jubilee USA Network**: Campaigns for cancellation of two-thirds-world debt

- **Medair**: Aids recovery of disaster-struck communities

- **A Rocha**: Conservation and environmental education

There are literally thousands more that could be mentioned. They range from multimillion-dollar organizations to anonymous missionaries working quietly in an obscure corner of the world. Christians obviously don't have a monopoly on socially beneficial, organized action. But the world as a whole benefits greatly from actions motivated by an understanding and experience of Jesus Christ.

Perhaps the best illustrations of outwards spirituality come from personal experience. Our home church, for example, helped start a food bank where low-income individuals can receive free sustenance. It's fed hundreds in our city. They didn't do this as a way to prove their outwards spirituality to others. But it is helpful to have such an example to share with friends who are spiritual but not religious. I'm sure you or your church have made similar efforts. Mentioning them can help break down the perception that the church's impact is all negative. However, if your church is not socially engaged it may struggle to attract those with an outwards spirituality.

Those with an outwards spiritual focus, then, may well assume that the church makes little positive contribution to the world. We should respond by sincerely admitting and apologizing for our failings in this area. But we can also challenge their perceptions by drawing on the vast array of examples from history, contemporary culture and personal experience. The world has consistently been impacted positively when people take Jesus seriously. Perhaps he's worth a second look?

CHRISTIAN TEACHINGS AND UPWARDS SPIRITUALITY

Christian teachings are another area producing uneasiness for people who are spiritual but not religious, especially those with an upwards dimension to their spirituality. A common assumption among many people who are spiritual but not religious is that doctrines and religious concepts limit one's spiritual development. "Religion is about belief and spirituality is about experience," as one person put it, and the two best not mix.[7]

Note that this is not a concern about the logical viability of the faith. It is, rather, a question about the practical, everyday value of Christian teachings. Our friends who are spiritual but not religious wonder whether these teachings facilitate a more effective upwards spirituality. If not, they conclude, then Christianity should be swiftly disregarded.

Our best response to such misgivings is to avoid abstract arguments. Instead, tell stories. Bring to life how the basics of the faith have enriched your own upwards spiritual experience. Do so in simple and honest terms with which your friends can relate.

You will likely have to tell stories in response to two kinds of questions:

Table 5.3

General Questions	Specific Questions
For example:	*For example:*
"Why have *any* beliefs?" "Does it matter what I believe?"	"Why worship a male deity?" "Aren't people essentially good?"

General questions relate to the value of even holding to *any* kind of teaching or belief. *Specific* questions focus on *a particular* teaching or doctrine that is perceived to hinder healthy spirituality. Responding to general questions is relatively straightforward. I recently had a chance to experience this with an engineer named Chris. I'd just finished interviewing him for a project with which I am involved, and then I discovered that he pursues an upwards form of spirituality. Prayer and meditation are an important part of his life.

Chris told me that he has engaged with many different religions and spiritual gurus. But he always loses interest when a given teacher starts explaining his or her theological or philosophical framework. He finds it incredibly limiting for these teachers to take an enormous concept such as spirituality and reduce it to words or doctrines. Don't we lose something significant when we squeeze expansive realities— God, the universe, the wonder of existence—into tiny little phrases or ideas, he wondered? It seems as futile as attempting to contain the ocean in a jam jar.

I nodded and expressed agreement. I then shared with him the story that I mentioned in chapter two about struggling to connect with the invisible God, that I used to do the same thing as him, trying to reach out to God through prayer. But for me it had always been a frustrating experience. I wondered to whom or what I was speaking. Sometimes I reveled in the mystery. Much of the time, though, the reality I sought kept slipping through my arms, and I wondered whether all I was doing was playing psychological tricks on myself.

Chris's eyes registered recognition, and he said firmly, "Yes, exactly, I feel this way too sometimes."

I said, "Well, here's the thing that really helped me with that. I was reading some of the ancient texts about Jesus, and I came across this famous line where he says that 'whoever has seen me has seen God.' In other words, if you want to see the personality and character of God, you need to look at Jesus' personality and character. I found that helpful. It wasn't saying 'know God through a concept or idea you can control,' but instead, look at this person and the stories of his life, and there you will find ultimate spiritual reality."

I continued, "There's a song which says about Jesus, 'He gave love a face, and he gave love a name,' and that's definitely been my experience. Reading the stories about him was the *starting point* for me of engaging true spiritual reality.[8] This didn't close off spiritual experience. It actually opened the door to it when I began praying to God as if he had the personality and character of Jesus."

Chris thought that was fascinating. So I asked him whether he'd ever looked into Jesus. He replied that he'd never really given Jesus much thought. This was all new to him. But he really liked the idea of seeing God through the lens of a person rather than an idea and thought maybe he should read the Jesus stories for himself.

This, then, is the most straightforward way to address general questions about the value of basic Christian beliefs and the concern that Christianity reduces God to concepts and doctrines: we reemphasize Jesus and stress that he didn't say, "This is the truth," but instead said, "I am the truth." Learning about God through the person and narrative of Jesus is quite a different experience from only understanding him through the prism of ideas.

It is common for people to see Christian beliefs as a distraction from authentic spiritual experience. Respond by describing how you have been impacted by God's self-revelation in Christ. Highlight how a focus on Jesus has ignited for you a richer spirituality rather than quenched it.

Note also that I did three things with Chris:

- Clarified his misunderstandings (that Christianity is fundamentally propositional)

- Narrated my experience (of encountering God in Christ)

- Posed a question (about whether he'd ever considered Jesus)

This three-step simple framework can be applied to almost any general or specific question we encounter. As an example, let's take one of the *specific* issues most commonly raised by upwardly spiritual people: Christian use of male imagery for God.

Many people outside the church think that Christians believe God is male. He is a Father. He has a Son. Clearly, they reason, he is a guy. He probably drives a pickup truck and smokes fat cigars while eating hearty steaks. Men have evidently created a masculine deity in their own image. But none of this is true. Not even the cigars. Especially not the bit about the gender of God. We will have to clear up this misunderstanding when it arises. We could do this quite easily by quoting some of the very first words in the Bible:

> So God created mankind in his own image,
>   in the image of God he created them;
>   male and female he created them. (Gen 1:27)

Both men and women, it seems, reflect something of the divine. We are all in his image. God is a person—a "he" rather than an "it"—and so are we. But he is not a man. There is plenty of female imagery used for God in the Bible. He is pained "like a woman in childbirth," protective as a mother "hen," as determined as a woman on a treasure hunt (Is 42:14; Mt 23:37; Lk 15:8-10). Male imagery dominates, for sure, but not because God is viewed as being gendered. One theologian explains that:

> [W]hen Christians call God "our Father," nothing is being said of God's gender, but only that . . . God gives life to believers . . . pro-tecting, training and disciplining us like a father with his children. . . . As with all metaphors, God may be Father in one sense but not in another. God describes himself as our Father because he acts like a father, first toward Jesus . . . and then toward us.[9]

The author highlights the aforementioned reference to God being like a mother hen. He wryly notes, "Our heavenly Father does not have the eternal attribute of divine masculinity any more than he has the eternal attribute of divine chickenhood."[10] Both are metaphors.[11]

You may well have to go into more depth than this. But it is surprising how often people simply haven't grasped basic aspects of

Christian theology, such as the nongendered nature of the Godhead. A few words can often clear these issues up. But we will need to step beyond clarification. We'll also need to narrate our experience and show the real-world value of what we are discussing. With conversations about male and female imagery of God, for example, we might want to share some of the ways in which conceiving of God as Father has helped us.

My wife, Whitney, for example, lost her earthly father at a young age. Larry Brown was a lovely man who cared deeply for his family. She has memories of him waking early and making pancakes for the family on Saturday mornings. He helped her with science projects and was involved and interested in all she did. When he passed away, she experienced an intense sense of loss. His absence tore away everything he had been—present, protective, caring and affirming—and left an enormous gap in her family's life.

Whitney had known God was called "the Father" from almost as early as she could understand words. But after her dad died, this imagery took on a whole new dimension for her. She says that the word *Father* began to convey that God was an unfailing, unlimited version of everything she had lost. His protection, presence, care and affirmation were deeper and more enduring than even a human parent could provide. The image of divine fatherhood painted God in vivid colors, which helped breathe life into her upwards spirituality.

You can likely come up with similar explanations of how biblical imagery of God, male or female, has enriched your own life. Tell those stories. But try not to monologue. Instead turn conversation into invitation. Open the door for them to enter imaginatively into what you share. Posing questions is a great way to do this. You might want to ask, for example, "If God were a person and not just a force or a power, what difference might that make for your spirituality?" or "If God could accurately be described as a Father, how might that reshape the way you live?" Then listen to their thoughts. These kinds of questions can help people process the possibilities that emerge from God being personal and father-like.

Such invitations to imagination can even open up some Jesus-flavored conversations. We don't have to manipulate them in that direction. They often unfold naturally along that route if we honestly share selected aspects of own experience and ask good questions.

It really helps bring Christian concepts to life, then, if we can communicate them to people in terms of their practical value and invite them to apply their imaginations to the questions being discussed. But we need to do this in conjunction with thoughtfully modifying their honest misunderstandings of what we believe.

BEYOND WORDS

Encountering the person and narrative of Jesus reorients people. This is evident in the social impact of his followers as well as in our personal experiences of him. Yet many self-professedly "spiritual" people have neither engaged with him nor hold positive impressions of the faith communities that bear his name. They seek to quench their thirst elsewhere. Through stories and examples, we can help unsettle this unchecked dismissal of Jesus. But people who are spiritual but not religious, with their desire for something beyond the ordinary, are unlikely to be impressed if all we can offer is words. We therefore turn next to some of the practices that can help make tangible the thirst-quenching nature of Jesus and his message.

TAKING IT FURTHER

Think of someone you know who would call him- or herself spiritual but not religious. Are they pursuing an upwards spirituality, an outwards one or a combination?

What is his or her number-one biggest misgiving about Christianity? Does the concern relate mainly to upwards or outwards matters?

What story from your own experience could you share that would address the concern you have identified?

PRACTICES

Inviting Others into an Experience of Christian Spirituality

Our own spirituality, especially the upwards aspect of it, is often sealed away from view when we interact with those outside the church. It's kept hidden from the spiritually thirsty in a sealed flask. We speak to them about the flask's contents, argue for it, explain it. But what's desperately required in this situation is much simpler: we need to unscrew the lid, pour them a glass and invite them to take a sip for themselves. We need to let them sample how Christian spirituality tastes and get an appetite for it. Otherwise it all feels like just words.

We often fail to make this move because we overlook the very existence of Christian spirituality. This hit me when I was talking with Nate, an education student at Bridgewater State University in Massachusetts. He told me how he had grown up going to church occasionally with his parents and had concluded that Christian spirituality—if it even existed—was all about obeying rules and attending church services. The most intense spiritual experience of his teens, he recalls, was attending a concert of alternative rock band

Third Eye Blind. He was especially swept up by the lyrics of their vintage song "Motorcycle Drive-By," which describes the profound internal wrestling of an idealistic person struggling with life:

> I've never been so alone
> And I've, I've never been so alive
> And there's this burning . . .
> Where's the soul I want to know.[1]

When Nate later became more active in his spiritual curiosity and began searching for "a way to live in tune with reality," the church was the last place he thought to look. Instead he listened to music, researched the zodiac and dabbled with Taoism and other East Asian philosophies encountered through books and friends. He told me that the very first time he attended a Christian meeting as an adult he was taken aback to be asked about his spiritual life by one of the leaders. He hadn't really expected anyone there to be remotely interested in spiritual experience or reality.

Nate's outlook is far from unique. Even Christians sometimes share it. One Christian friend of mine managed to construct an entire university syllabus on the spirituality of the major religions without including an introduction to Christian spirituality. He, like many others, overlooked that the heart of Christianity includes a distinctive vision of both upwards and outwards spirituality.

Indonesian theologian Armand Barus says that one of the main features of Christian spirituality is that the "vertical relationship determines the nature of the horizontal relationship."[2] Outwards spirituality, in other words, flows from an upwards experience of God.

Different groups and denominations stress different aspects of this experience of God. Just visit a Pentecostal church and a Roman Catholic parish over the next two Sundays and you'll see what I mean. Yet for all the different accents within sections of the church, there is a common emphasis that underpins the life of every Christian group. Theologian Simon Chan summarizes this shared focal point:

Christian spirituality may be defined as life lived in relationship with the God who reveals himself in Jesus Christ through the Holy Spirit. Since the triune God is essentially persons-in-relationship, Christian spirituality sees ... the central expression of the Christian life [as] . . . essentially relationship with the triune God and with one another in a community characterized by self-giving love.[3]

As we participate in the life of the Trinity—relating to the Father, through the Son, in the power of the Spirit—we also become God's partners in expressing his love to one another and to the wider world. This life is rooted in the context of the church family, nurtured by the sacraments and shaped by the guidance of Scripture. This, as I'm sure you'll recognize, is the bare bones of what is taught by every church you've ever encountered. It's so hidden in plain sight that many of us don't even register it as a distinctive spirituality at all. Yet it is quite unlike what is being pursued by our friends who are spiritual but not religious.

All three practices you'll encounter in this chapter are designed to unscrew the lid on the flask of basic Christian spirituality so it can be sipped by others. Nicole, Greg and Andrew—each of whom you're about to meet—have discovered simple, replicable ways of inviting people into their upwards and outwards spirituality. Through following their examples you can help Jesus to become more tangible, desirable and plausible to your spiritually thirsty friends.

MINI PRACTICE: PERSONAL OPENNESS

One of the best practitioners of an open and inviting spirituality is my friend Nicole Voelkel. We met while studying together in Chicago and continue to regularly cross paths in different settings. I'm always struck by the readiness with which she invites others into an experience of God.

Once such memorable moment occurred while we sat in a Wisconsin pub drinking beer with some friends. Nicole suddenly pushed her chair back from the table, excused herself and walked to a nearby table to engage its occupants in conversation. Soon I saw her with her hand on one of their shoulders. She was clearly praying. The stranger she was touching had his eyes closed and his head bowed.

After a few minutes she wandered back over to our table, sat down and took another sip of her beer. "Sorry about that," she said. "I just felt that I needed to go and pray for him." She'd told him that she had something encouraging to share with him. Then she let him know what God had prompted her to say. It was so precise a word for his life that he immediately burst into tears, and so she asked whether she could pray for him.

These kinds of incidents are normal with Nicole. She doesn't hide her upwards spirituality. Even in settings such as bars and pubs she is guilelessly open about her relationship with God. It's a way of life that is tremendously attractive to all kinds of people, especially those who describe themselves as spiritual but not religious. We don't need to hide that we are praying people with a connection to a real, living God. We are inviting people to a truer spiritual experience that can be demonstrated as well as described.

I recently asked Nicole to tell me more about how she approaches people to speak about Jesus. She replied that I had asked the wrong question. Instead, she said that speaking about Jesus is only secondarily about how we approach people. It is primarily about how we interact with the Holy Spirit. We should seek to follow the Spirit's leading and prompting as he draws us to the right people. God will then infuse our words and actions with an appropriateness and power we couldn't muster purely through our own effort and planning.

Nicole often tells a story about one of her early experiences of following the Spirit's leading. It happened while she was splitting her time between working for a school district in Chicago and training with a semiprofessional triathlon team. She was pondering whether God still heals today and felt that she should pray aloud *with* the next one hundred people who told her they were ill or injured.

Her early efforts were hurried and embarrassed. She'd be chatting after training or in the office and discover that a colleague was unwell. Her response would be to rapidly mutter something like, "Oh, you've got a bad back, let me pray for you, Jesus please heal them, amen, bye," and then scuttle quickly away. The interactions terrified her.

Slowly, though, she relaxed into it. By the thirtieth time, people began being healed on the spot. Her boss was cured of a painful, ongoing leg ailment. Some of the recipients of her earlier hurried prayers were also coming back and telling her they felt better after her prayers. These occurrences opened up many conversations about Jesus and marked the birth of Nicole's current manner of communicating about him.

The first time I heard Nicole tell this story I dismissed its potential as a model to follow myself. As I reflected further, though, it occurred to me that everything she was doing reflected simple New Testament priorities shared by all followers of Jesus. The Holy Spirit lives in us. Every Christian believes this means the Spirit can tangibly work through us. Few of us, however, act on this belief the same way Nicole did in her office.

When Nicole and I were sharing the platform at a university student conference I could see the skepticism cross everyone's faces as she told her stories about healing. So I asked the audience, "How many of you present have ever prayed *with*—and not just for— someone who is not a Christian?" Just one hand went up. I then suggested to them, "Maybe the issue here is not that this can't happen but that we've never even taken the risk to see if it might." It's not a question of whether we consider ourselves "charismatic" or not. It's more about whether we are prepared to apply our private convictions about God answering prayer in everyday situations.

There are dangers in Nicole's approach. She says, for example, that people who are spiritual but not religious often "collect" transcendent experiences. They see God at work, think it's cool, then place what happened on the shelf next to all the other spiritual encounters from their past. They therefore need well-focused words about Jesus to help them distinguish what they see in Christians from what they might have encountered elsewhere.

Nicole shared her top five tips for those who want to be more attractive and open to people seeking spiritual satisfaction:

- **Encounter God.** Set aside regular time for connecting personally with him. A vibrant relationship with God will naturally overflow into all of life. It also keeps you attuned to his voice and ready to respond to his leading.

- **Meditate on Scripture.** This is the best way to hear from God. You'll be surprised how often something you just read ends up being the perfect thing to share with someone you meet. Regular immersion in Scripture is like a daily trip to the bakery; it means you always have "fresh bread" with which to feed your spiritually hungry friends.

- **Stay curious.** Don't judge people or place them in mental boxes. Instead, cultivate a genuine curiosity about them. God is already at work in their lives. Ask good questions and listen well to figure out what he's been doing with them.

- **Ask God questions.** Nicole often asks God, "how do you see this person?" or "how is this person meant to be?" These kinds of prayers allow God to shape our thinking even as we are interacting with people.

- **Embody Jesus.** Think about what Jesus would say to each person. Consider what might be his tone of voice and manner. Ensure that your interactions with others don't just mention Jesus but instead reflect his character and attitude.

Inviting others to follow Jesus, then, requires that we ourselves are in ongoing communication with him. We can hardly invite others into a truer upwards spiritual experience if we are walking at a distance from him. If our relationship with Christ is current and alive, then we will have a spirituality into which we can invite others.

MESO PRACTICE: INVITATION TO ACTION

Upwards spirituality isn't the only aspect of Christian experience into which we can invite others. Our outwards spirituality, lovingly embracing the world God made, can also be the means through which the possibility of following Jesus becomes more accessible to others.

Outwards spirituality is a key part of Greg Johnson's life. Greg travels every year to New Orleans with a combined team of Christians and others. They spend their time working on various rebuilding projects that sprang up in the devastating aftermath of 2005's Hurricane Katrina. Greg says these trips provide the best opportunities he's ever experienced to express to others what it means to follow Jesus.

His involvement in New Orleans began almost as an accidental byproduct of his work with InterVarsity Christian Fellowship's college ministry in Rhode Island and Massachusetts. For years New England InterVarsity staff had been taking groups of students down south to build homes with Habitat for Humanity during spring break. The InterVarsity students began inviting along friends who weren't Christians. The road trip experience, serving together and the InterVarsity students being open about their faith proved to be an attractive combination for all who came.

But it was only after Katrina that Greg began to realize the full possibilities of such cooperative projects. Their first visit to Louisiana came not long after the partial destruction of the city by unprecedented storms. Greg explained to me that the bleakness of the situation "knocked down the door" on the students' previously comfortable worldviews and triggered "a deep hunger for a better world, a desire which they struggled to explain." It made them long, in other words, for the kingdom of God; the reign of Jesus curating our world into peace and wholeness. The bridge from wishing for the kingdom to following the King was a short one that many students traversed.

Not all partnership projects have to be so dramatic. Nor must they be confined to short visits. My friend Joey Espinosa recently spent four years living in a run-down neighborhood of underresourced

Allendale County in South Carolina. He moved there from the cozy, upstate corner where he previously worked as a chemist and then a children's pastor. Joey and his wife, Joanna, served in Allendale with a range of people from outside the church to implement mentoring programs and afterschool clubs intended to raise the education prospects of local teenagers. All this while trying to parent three young kids and hold down as many as four jobs simultaneously.

Their efforts brought them into contact with many locals who were excited that somebody wanted to invest in Allendale's children. Every project they initiated included a mix of Christians and others. Joey says he didn't really think of it as a strategy for reaching outwardly spiritual people. His aim was just to invest in the community, to "love because he first loved us" (1 Jn 4:19). But he has found doing so opened up a regular stream of conversations about Jesus with people who would otherwise dismiss both Jesus and the church.

Joey continues to pursue justice in the company of anyone available to help. He told me that he's happy to just plow on with doing good and let discussion about Jesus arise spontaneously. Greg, on the other hand, is more intentional. He believes there is a "secret sauce," a set of essential ingredients, which help others effectively implement cooperative projects with those who reflect an outwards spirituality.

I think both Greg's and Joey's approaches—the spontaneous and the planned—are valid options. Most of us probably lean more toward one than the other. But, even if we are more Joey than Greg, we can benefit by learning from someone with a different emphasis. So I asked Greg whether he might be willing to share the recipe for his secret sauce with me. He was more than happy to do so and said there are six main ingredients:

- **Be upfront about your aims.** Don't get anyone involved through false pretenses. Greg tells people he is inviting them to "a diverse learning community made up of people of different spiritual backgrounds, exploring the intersection between justice, spirituality and the Christian faith." Make sure you are similarly as honest about what you're up to.

- **Do meaningful work.** You're aiming to authentically express an outwards Christian spirituality. So do things that make a difference. Don't just undertake token projects that make you feel as though you are doing something but have no impact on others. We want our team and other people and settings to be affected for the better by what happens.

- **Build on existing relationships.** The best people to invite along are those with whom you already have trust and friendship. Working together on the project will then just be the next step in a story that began before your trip and will continue after it ends.

- **Interweave service and reflection.** It's important to do the work together. But it is also essential to create space to step back and process what's going on. Let people have room to think through all that they are seeing and feeling. Greg says that he used to have nightly team times where he would read a passage from the life of Jesus and offer a few thoughts for contemplation and discussion. One particularly memorable such occasion came after a draining day in the decaying post-Katrina streets. Greg read the story of Lazarus being raised from the dead and asked everyone to ponder, "Where does the power come from to resurrect a world like ours from death to life?" The relevance of Jesus had rarely been more intensely felt by most of those present.

- **Relinquish control.** Recognize that God will work differently with each individual. Be available and open to speak with everyone. But don't attempt to control their spiritual journeys. They each need freedom to engage with God and process their experiences in their own unique way.

- **Debrief with interpretive small groups.** Don't just send everybody home when you're done. Reserve at least a day at the end of the project to collectively interpret what people have experienced. Form small groups where participants can share honestly. Ensure that at least one member of each group is well prepared to guide the discussion and to help participants make sense of what it all means for them.

All of these are helpful pointers. Inviting others into our expressions of outwards spirituality can be an important step to help them discover Jesus. We can facilitate this process if we find a way to combine meaningful work with space to reflect on Jesus.

MACRO PRACTICE: CREATIVE RITUALS

Larger church gatherings are often a missed opportunity for engaging people who are spiritual but not religious. Singing, speaking and sacraments are the elements of most church gatherings. Some traditions may also include liturgy. But if a visitor isn't into music then the opportunity for him or her to actively sample Christian spirituality is often limited to listening to a talk and saying "Amen" after a prayer.

My friend Andrew Givens says that this reality can severely limit our capacity to reach the spiritually curious. He first experienced this problem while he was planting a Christian community on the campus of the University of North Carolina Wilmington. The Carolinas are located in an area where the legacy of segregation still hangs thick in the air. So Andrew prioritized the development of a multiethnic chapter of InterVarsity Christian Fellowship on campus.

It was hard work at first. But a group slowly emerged composed of around seventy white, black and Latino students. Students of all ethnicities soon began inviting their friends to attend the large group meetings. These newcomers were especially impressed by the unusual levels of interracial harmony they encountered. Their curiosity was piqued by this glimpse of outwards Christian spirituality. But few began following Jesus.

So the InterVarsity leaders began pondering possible means of inviting these visitors into an upwards experience of God. They weren't starting from scratch; each main meeting featured a biblical text that students discussed in small groups. But what the students needed was space for everyone to pause and hear the voice of the Spirit in these passages a little more clearly.

They eventually developed a concept they called "prayer prompts." These often followed a basic four-step pattern:

1. After the group discussed the Scripture passage, everyone closed their eyes and imagined themselves within the passage. For example, after examining Jesus' invitation in Luke 5 for three fishermen to follow him, Andrew invited those present to picture the scene on the seashore, feel the stones beneath their feet and turn to look at the boats they were about to leave behind (Lk 5:1-11).

2. The leader offered a question for everyone to consider. In the session on the three fishermen, for example, Andrew focused on the last line of the passage: "So they pulled their boats up on shore, left everything and followed him" (Lk 5:11). He asked, "What is your 'everything' in your boat, that Jesus may be asking you to leave behind?" Then the students were given a time of silence to reflect on the question.

3. The leader encouraged everyone present to pray and ask whether God had a word or a picture for them to share with someone else in the room. After the Luke 5 discussion several of the newcomers were surprised to then be approached by someone who had received a very accurate and personal message to share with them. The same Spirit who inspired the text was now addressing them individually. They experienced a tangible expression of upwards Christian spirituality.

4. The leader closed with a short presentation tying together the God they just experienced with the passage discussed earlier in the meeting, all culminating in an invitation for personal response. Andrew's concluding words at the session on the three fisherman resulted in five people beginning a new life with Jesus, which is still ongoing a year later. Twenty-nine more students

made similar lasting commitments in the subsequent few months, which was a huge outcome for a relatively small and newly planted Christian community.

I was reminded, as Andrew shared this with me, of how theologian John Goldingay describes communication about God:

> Let us imagine that God is like a lion, as the Old Testament says. . . . Testimony is then like telling people you have met a lion. Preaching is like inviting people to come and meet a lion. Theology is like reflecting on your meeting with the lion.[4]

I asked Andrew whether it would be accurate to describe the "prayer prompts" as inviting the lion into the room and letting people hear it roar in their presence. Andrew replied, "You know, I probably wouldn't say it like that; it's not like we bring God into a room when we pray or speak for him, so I would actually describe it as being that the lion is *already in the room*. It's just that we're distracted by other things and haven't noticed. Our prayer prompts are a way to bring back that awareness of the lion's presence."

I asked Andrew for his top advice for people who want to learn from his experience. He identified two simple but vital starting factors:

- **Leaders are key.** They must be regularly listening to God's voice, both through Scripture and also more directly, or they cannot lead others in doing the same. Expecting to "turn it on" as a performance in Christian meetings is a recipe for powerlessness and failure. Andrew therefore prioritizes helping his student leaders be consistently attentive and responsive to the Holy Spirit's leading in their own lives.

- **Try things out.** Andrew wouldn't suggest you copy what he does. Pray and think about what might make upwards Christian spirituality accessible and inviting to the people you know who need Jesus. Then test some of those ideas in an upcoming gathering. The main aim in any meeting, Andrew told me, is that people should "come and see who the Lord is." The exact shape of how we do that can vary endlessly.

Andrew offers great advice. The lion is already crouching in the corner of every room in which we meet. Yet we can be so busy following our established patterns that people can visit our main meetings without ever noticing his presence. Developing a group of leaders who know God's voice and who can teach others to do the same is a great starting point. Then try a little experimentation and wait for that pivotal moment when people begin feeling the lion's breath on the back of their necks for the first time.

OPENING THE FLASK

None of the practices in this chapter require we do anything radically new. We all already pray, attend regular Christian meetings and work for the good of others. What we need to discover, though, is how to make it *easy* for others to join us in these activities. Nicole, Greg and Andrew have all witnessed the impact that follows when we do. So too has Nate, the spiritually inquisitive Bridgewater State University student we met earlier.

Nate's assumption that "Christian spirituality" was an oxymoron began to crumble after he connected with Erin, a follower of Jesus and an InterVarsity colleague of Greg Johnson. She would stop and chat with him about his spiritual life whenever they ran into each other on campus. She spoke openly of her own relationship with God and took a genuine interest in Nate's existential meanderings. Erin was the first Christian who had ever opened the door on her own spiritual life to Nate.

During one of these occasional conversations, Erin mentioned to Nate that she would soon be helping lead a team down to Tampa. It would be a service trip, helping impoverished communities, and Erin's Christian community was leading it. She suggested he join them. Nate thought, "Why not?" and signed up.

On the first day of the Tampa trip Nate found himself working on a construction project under the direction of a former drug addict who kept saying things such as "Jesus saved me" and "God loves you." Nate says these phrases, which seemed to mean everything to the man, sounded like gibberish to his ears. Yet he was impressed by what he saw of the Christians and became more open to considering Jesus with every day he spent serving alongside them.

Nate's curiosity kept growing until eventually he took Erin aside and asked, "Do you really think there's a bearded man in the clouds answering all your prayers?" Erin sat down with him and explained what Christians really believe about God. Nate admitted to her his confusion as to what *he* believed, so Erin challenged him: "Why don't you pray?" He said he probably should sometime. Erin replied, "No, let's do it now!" and so Nate found himself unexpectedly praying for the first time in his life. He sincerely asked God to show him whether or not he is real.

Nate didn't have to wait long for an answer to his prayer. At 4:30 the next morning, while everyone was asleep on air mattresses in a big hall, another student awoke screaming with a terror unlike any Nate had ever heard. Everyone opened their groggy eyes in surprise. A dark energy seemed to fill the room. Leaders calmed the student down, and he went back to sleep only to wake again with a blood-chilling shriek. He only settled for the night after a group of students came together to pray for him. Peace returned, and everybody went back to sleep.

But things didn't stay calm for long. During dinner the next evening Nate unexpectedly began to feel as anxious as he had during the previous night's screaming. He wandered to the sleeping quarters seeking rest. Instead he found himself gripped by horror as inanimate objects began to transform before his eyes. A Timberland boot appeared to him like a dead man's face. He'd never been so scared in his life. So, for the second time in his life, he prayed to God. Instantly he sensed a warmth and peace around him, and the terrifying images and sense of fear disappeared. This was even more surprising to Nate than the scary visions. He began to think that perhaps God was real after all.

Over the following days all the confusing statements of his supervisor began to make sense. Phrases like "God loves you" and "Jesus saved me" became filled with meaning as he spent time working alongside Christians each day and experienced God in prayer. On the penultimate night of the service trip, he approached Erin and told her what had been happening. After listening carefully to his story, she had just one question: "Are you ready to follow Jesus now?" He nodded and she burst into tears. They sat to pray together and, as they did so, three words flashed before Nate's eyes: "heaven on earth." He was entering the spiritual reality he had been seeking for so long. And the catalyst for it all was a community of Christians willing to unscrew the lid off their own spirituality and offer him a sip.

TAKING IT FURTHER

Are you tempted to keep your spiritual experience hidden from view when you interact with those outside the church? Pause for a moment to think why this might be.

How could you unscrew the lid on the flask of your spirituality this week? What aspect of Christian spirituality could you most easily make accessible to others? Take a moment to ask God to show you the first step to doing this in your situation, and note what you discern in the space below:

STORIES

Dawkins on a Bike (and Other Tales)

two men sit by the window of a café. One asks the other, "What's more important . . . to explain science or destroy religion?"

Without hesitation his friend replies, "Oh, I think they go together. Destroying religion makes it sound negative, but to me it is a positive thing . . . religion is not wonderful, it's not beautiful; it gets in the way."

I'm looking on with bemusement. The scene is unfolding on my television as I watch a DVD of the documentary movie *The Unbelievers*.[1] Later in the film the two men from the café take turns standing on a stage before a vast sea of people at an outdoor rally. One of them is applauded rapturously when he declares that Christians should be openly mocked for their beliefs. The other receives an ovation for his call to put an end to religious ways of thinking. As they tour talk shows and universities around the world, the pair announce that belief in God is experiencing "the beginning of its death throes" and will soon begin to fade from the scene.

The Unbelievers is just one in a long line of documentaries, books, podcasts and websites that have emerged in recent years promoting a particularly hostile approach to religion and to the idea of God. This movement is known as New Atheism. *The Unbeliever's* stars, Richard Dawkins and Lawrence Krauss, are two of its leading figures.[2]

THE NEW ATHEISM

Atheism—"the belief that there is no God or gods"—is hardly a new development; there have always been people who have held such a viewpoint.[3] But Dawkins and others have adopted an unprecedentedly aggressive tone that characterizes all religion as "irrational" and "dangerous."[4] They are out to crush all belief in God.

The first time I saw Richard Dawkins in person was while I was a student at Oxford University. Some friends and I had arrived early at the Oxford Union to watch a public debate about the existence of God between some lesser-known atheists and Christians. We were waiting for the doors to open when a familiar long-faced figure with thinning gray hair walked around the corner and shuffled slowly past us: Dawkins, a professor at the university.

Two thoughts went through my head in rapid succession. The first was, "Oh no, it's the Dark Lord!" As a Christian, I felt as though Darth Vader or Harry Potter's evil nemesis, Voldemort, had wandered casually through the room. It was a surreal moment.

The second thought was quite different. I suddenly saw him as a person, just an old man with wrinkly skin and imperfect hair. I had become so accustomed to thinking of Dawkins as the enemy of Christians and the omnipresent media face of New Atheism that I had dehumanized him. But there he was looking like somebody's grandfather on an evening out.

The second time I saw him was a few months later. My Nigerian friend Gideon and I had just attended a lecture on animal rights by a well-known atheist philosopher. Though Gideon and I both believe in the compassionate treatment of animals, we were enraged by the reasoning used by the lecturer to support his case. He was casual about whether it was acceptable to kill children in infancy and said that we should assess the comparative value of crabs and human babies by measuring each one's relative capacity to feel pain.

As we walked down a leafy Oxford street, Gideon and I were tag-teaming on full-blown rants against the lecturer and against atheism in general. We were angry that this kind of thinking was becoming an intellectually acceptable viewpoint among students and professors. Outrageous ideas, we agreed, were becoming legitimized simply because erudite and educated men in suits say them in measured sentences to academic audiences. I felt that the prominence of New Atheists like Dawkins had opened the door to such ideas being respected in the city.

At the very moment my tirade against Dawkins began to hit full stride, a bicycle whizzed past us. On it was a man in his seventies wearing a protective helmet. Richard Dawkins was again making a cameo appearance in my life.

Once more an unexpected thought entered my mind. This time it was a Bible verse: "For we wrestle not against flesh and blood, but . . . against the rulers of the darkness of this world" (Eph 6:12 KJV). Then it hit me: Dawkins was not the man we were fighting. Nor was the philosopher we just heard lecture. Their arguments certainly need addressing. But they are as much casualties of the ideas they promote as anybody else.

ASSEMBLY OF THE SKEPTICAL

Not all atheists are quite so hostile to religion as Richard Dawkins. Some are so friendly to it that they incorporate large chunks of it into their own practice.

I recently experienced this firsthand. It was shortly before 11 a.m. on a Sunday morning, and I was in my seat waiting for a meeting to start. A band was warming up in one corner of the stage and a choir was practicing in the other. In a few minutes the music would kick off and everyone would begin bouncing and swaying as they sang. Some would close their eyes and lift their arms in the air. Others would dance in the aisles. In between songs, we would hear a rousing message about forgiveness from a visiting speaker, listen to testimonies of members who had experienced the healing power of forgiving others and all bow our heads in a moment of silent reflection and meditation. At the end there would be coffee, cake and a table where newcomers could sign up to join a small group.

As I waited for the meeting to begin I looked at the screen above the stage and saw a slide entitled "Our Mission," which read, "To help everyone find and fulfill their potential." It wasn't much different from many churches' mission statements. The next slide, though, was unlike any I'd ever seen. It read: "Our Vision: A godless congregation in every town, city and village that wants one." You read that right; a movement that plants "godless" congregations.

I was at the Sunday Assembly. It's a worldwide network that launches communities and gatherings that look a whole lot like church. The big difference, though, is that Sunday Assemblies don't believe in God. They are atheistic. They sing classic songs by the Beatles and Tracy Chapman, and listen to TED-style talks that assume a God-free view of the world. You can find Sunday Assemblies at a growing list of locations, including cities in the heart of the Bible Belt such as Atlanta, Nashville and Birmingham.

The Sunday Assembly appeals to a broad crowd. The day of my visit to the Sunday Assembly there were more than three hundred people of all ages present. I sat next to two young women who had arrived together and asked them why they had come. One told me she grew up going to a Christian school and missed the ritual of Sunday morning attendance. It was nice to find a place where she could do this without the God stuff, she said. Her friend, who was described to me as "a bit of an evangelist for the Sunday Assembly," said that she had no religious background and just found the event and its rituals a refreshing focal point for her life.

When Christians hear about the Sunday Assembly, I have heard them say things like, "Ah well, it seems that atheists are effectively acknowledging that they really need what we have to offer." I'm not so sure, however, that it's accurate to view these assemblies as back-handed compliments to Christianity. Of course, it's lovely that this brand of atheism is more amicable towards some aspects of religion. None of us wants hostility or anger to pervade our interactions with others. But the core convictions of the Sunday Assembly are actually quite similar to those of Dawkins and friends. Along with most Western forms of atheism over the past several hundred years, they both insist that all of life can be explained without reference to God or anything transcendent. Atheism—the viewpoint that God most likely does not exist—tends to posit material and physical explanations for all of life. When they borrow from religion, therefore, atheists are not affirming any aspect of Christian belief. They are instead attempting to "burn off [Christianity's] more dogmatic aspects in order to distill a few aspects of [it] that could prove timely and consoling to skeptical minds . . . to rescue some of what is beautiful, touching and wise from all that no longer seems true."[5]

New Atheism and the Sunday Assembly are just two contemporary expressions of atheism. They don't necessarily reflect the attitudes of all contemporary atheists. But, like the temple-goers at Burning Man (mentioned in chapter four), they offer us a vivid and more sharply focused version of an understanding and approach to life that exists in hazy tones all around us.

FLAVORS OF ATHEISM

Atheism is actually a very diverse phenomenon that encompasses a wide range of people. Many Christians assume that all atheists are probably similar to one another and therefore also quite unlike the average follower of Jesus. Research suggests, however, that there are very few demographic differences between believers in God ("theists") and atheists.[6]

Take a look at table 7.1. The academics who compiled these statistics note that the major variations between atheists and believers in God (their rates of marriage and average number of children) are probably due to atheists typically being marginally younger and thus having "had less time to marry and have children."[7] The two groups are otherwise very alike.[8]

When we hear a person describe themselves as "atheist," then, we should hold back on assuming that this tells us anything about their values, social background, work ethic or politics. There is as much range among atheists as there is among believers in God, and we'll need to get to know them each as individuals. We'll obviously meet some atheists who are quite different from us. But many will be very similar. You simply won't be able to spot most atheists just by looking at them or their lifestyles.

Table 7.1

	Atheists in the US	Theists in the US
Average Age	38	44
Political Views (1=left, 10=right)	5	6
Environmentally Concerned	51%	57%
Satisfaction with Life (1=low, 10=high)	7	8
Married	38%	56%
Cohabiting	6%	5%
Divorced	10%	9%
Average Number of Children	1	2
Middle Class	64%	64%
Working Class	31%	32%

There is also great variety in the reasons why people are atheists. Martin Smith, whom we met in chapter three, firmly believed that faith in God is irrational and absurd. His was a fundamentally intellectual conviction regarding the unreasonableness of Christian beliefs. Other atheists, however, have much more complex motives for disaffirming the existence of God.

A recent set of studies published by *The Journal of Personality and Social Psychology*, for example, revealed that anger toward God is common even among atheists.[9] Julie Exline, the psychology professor who led the research, records that "those who endorsed their religious beliefs as 'atheist/agnostic' or 'none/unsure' reported more anger toward God than those who reported a religious affiliation."[10]

This suggests that some people may deny the existence of God because they feel he has failed them or is blameworthy in various ways. They would prefer he not exist. We should be aware, then, that some atheists' intellectual objections to God may be accompanied and possibly fueled by a sense of unfulfilled expectation toward him. One atheist blogger describes how some Christian friends lost two young children in separate car accidents. He says that he feels more anger toward God than his Christian friends about these deaths:

> I'm the atheist . . . but I want to be angry at God, even though he doesn't exist. I want to be angry at God for not protecting [these] children. For causing so much pain and hurt to [their parents]. For not being there for the people who are supposed to be your followers and believers.[11]

Still other atheists have a quite relaxed attitude toward God. They may even have a comfortable relationship with the church. Venture capitalist Nigel Hamway stopped believing in God during his teens while attending a church-run school. He still loves the New Testament documents, though, and in a recent interview described warmly how Western culture "is shaped by the Christian story, the incarnation and the death and resurrection of Christ and by the ethical values encapsulated in that narrative."[12] He continues to attend church with his wife and children, and has even written an Easter song, "Christ is Risen," which has been sung several times by his local congregation.[13] He just doesn't buy into the idea that a real God actually underpins all these things. Hence he is an atheist.

Most atheists, though, are neither religious nor angry. They may not even have given their atheism much thought at all. When speaking at universities I often end up in conversation with students who introduce themselves to me as atheist. A few minutes into our interactions, however, it frequently becomes clear that "atheist" is just shorthand for "not particularly religious or aware of any evidence for the existence of God." It is a label adopted by many people in the absence of any suitable alternative.

We should be cautious, then, in assuming that we know what a person means when they say they are "atheist." A wide range of people do not believe in God and they do so for a variety of reasons. Some will have been inspired by the likes of Dawkins, others motivated by communities like the Sunday Assembly, but most will simply have made their own path to atheism through some combination of intellectual questioning, emotional unrest, religious involvement and lack of alternative options.

ALTERNATIVE LABELS

Not all atheists use the term *atheist* to describe their outlook. Some might call themselves skeptics, free thinkers, brights, rationalists, irreligious, secularists, naturalists, physicalists, materialists, agnostics, humanists or something else altogether. Others might not use any label. It's only by listening to the individual we can move past simple categorizations and begin to grasp the nuances of what they really believe.

Not So Far

The public prominence of New Atheism—probably the only strand of atheism that currently receives significant media exposure—has caused many public discussions about God to become angry and confrontational. Conflict-adverse Christians can therefore easily run and hide from engagement with atheists. More confident believers take the opposite approach and adopt a rhetoric and tone that matches that of Dawkins and his friends. Neither of these responses, either stridency or avoidance, are ideal responses to atheism. We need a better way.

It may be helpful for us to learn from other Christians who have had to interact with widespread atheism for far longer than has been the case for many of us in the West. Tomáš Halík, for example, was a leader in the Czech underground church during his nation's years under an oppressive dictatorship. Few knew he was an ordained Roman Catholic priest, and even his theological studies occurred in secret. Popular revolutions around the region in the late 1980s led to new democracies, and in many nearby countries religious revivals broke out as Christians were permitted to proclaim Jesus publicly for the first time in decades. The Czech Republic, though, bucked this trend and experienced a near-total collapse in religious belief. Just 16 percent of all Czechs now profess to believe in God, the lowest rate in all of Europe.[14]

Halík is well-placed, then, to offer insights into atheism and its relationship to the Christian faith. We might expect him to have an angry and combative attitude toward the atheism that has displaced the previously dominant Catholicism in his own country. One European Christian, for example, dismisses atheists as "the most colossally smug and annoying people on the planet."[15] Halík's approach, however, is much warmer and more conciliatory.

The Bible, Halík points out, is full of themes of God's apparent absence. The seeming hiddenness of God is a common theme among the Prophets. Some scholars identify the apparent absence of God as one of the major motifs of the Jewish and Christian Scriptures. When an atheist says they see insufficient evidence for God or they are frustrated at a sense of his failing them, then they are picking up a theme already in the foundational texts of the very religions with which they purport to disagree.

Jesus, in fact, cried out on the cross, "My God, my God, why have you forsaken me?" It was a moment when he sensed and experienced his Father's absence. G. K. Chesterton reflects quite strikingly on Jesus' desolated shout during his crucifixion, writing: "Let the atheists themselves choose a god. They will find only one divinity who ever uttered their isolation; only one religion in which God seemed for an instant to be an atheist."[16]

Even Jesus himself once felt that God was absent. This is provocative stuff. Even if we feel uncomfortable with Chesterton's exact phrasing, this should give us pause before we are unsympathetic ourselves toward atheists.[17] It certainly means that we need to abandon an antagonistic stance toward those who don't believe in God. Atheism is, Halík writes, not best conceived of as the photo negative of Christianity.

Figure 7.1

He suggests instead that atheism and Christianity may be more helpfully understood as points along a continuum.

Figure 7.2

What separates one from the other? According to Halík, "patience is . . . the main difference between faith and atheism." He writes,

I agree with atheists on many things, often on almost every-thing—except their belief that God doesn't exist. In today's bus-tling marketplace of religious wares of every kind, I sometimes feel closer with my Christian faith to the skeptics or to the atheist or agnostic critics of religion. With certain kinds of atheists I share a sense of God's absence from the world. However, I regard their interpretation of this feeling as too hasty, as an expression of impatience.[18]

God can sometimes seem absent. He certainly is not always obvious to us. But just because he is not immediately obvious doesn't mean he is not real, available or knowable.

Halík is not suggesting that the patience of Christians marks them as more virtuous than their atheistic counterparts. He is simply pointing out that it is a biblical theme—and an experienced reality even for most Christians—that God's reality is not always instanta-neously or easily graspable. Remembering this helps Christians in-teract with atheists with both kindness and understanding.

NOT EVERYTHING REAL IS OBVIOUS

Many important things in our world are not instantly compre-hensible. During the course of every day, for example, I see the sun move slowly across the sky as if it were doing a fly-over. It seems to be circling the Earth. It is only when I take the time to move past first appearances by investigating our so-lar system that I discover the Earth is actually revolving around the sun, contrary to what initially seems so obvious.

OPEN TO RECONSIDER

Christians, then, should be sympathetic to atheists. They should also be aware that atheists may not have had as much direct experience of

Christianity as they might assume. Degree of firsthand religious experience, in fact, stands out as *the* major difference between a typical believer in God and the average atheist. Research reveals that:

43% of US atheists were raised religious

84% of US theists were raised religious[19]

Atheists, it seems, are half as likely as believers in God to have had *any* religious background. This is not to say that all atheists are warm and positive toward Christianity. The New Atheists certainly are not. But in a majority of cases, it's possible that an atheist's perceptions of religion are shaped by something other than the actual teachings and beliefs of Christians. This will inevitably lead to honest misunderstandings regarding basic elements of Christianity. Part of our role in engaging the concerns of atheists is therefore to clarify what Christians actually do believe.

Even the nation that gave the world Richard Dawkins is not immune to the pull of the transcendent. Research undertaken in the United Kingdom shows that people with a college education are more likely to convert *from* atheism *to* belief in God than to move in the opposite direction. Possessing a master's degree pushes up the odds of their rejection of atheism even further.[20]

Christians therefore should not interact with atheists as if they are hardened and close-minded. When engaging with the question of God for themselves, they may well change their minds. But to help them make an informed decision we will need to have thoughtfully considered their questions and concerns for ourselves. (We turn to this topic in the next chapter.)

Atheists are a diverse bunch. Between the ritualized practices of the Sunday Assembly and the bombastic rhetoric of the New Atheism lies a wide range of other, less publicly visible shades of atheist. These include people who default to atheism through lack of apparent alternatives, those who run to it out of disappointment with God and others who appreciate Christianity but simply can't accept its basic teachings. As we seek to engage our atheist friends and family we will need to display the kind of patience mentioned by Tomáš Halík. God is not instantly obvious to all. But as they encounter Christ in our lives and our words, thoughtful atheists may become open to reconsidering whether he offers a glimpse of divinity that is both plausible and desirable.

TAKING IT FURTHER

Have you ever thought or spoken ill of atheists? Take a moment to repent of your unloving attitude and pray for a kinder and more loving attitude toward them.

Check out some atheist writings online (for example, the Atheist portal at Patheos) and have a firsthand look at contemporary atheist bloggers.[21] Find a couple of article titles that grab your attention and read with care. Try to identify areas of agreement as well as disagreement. See what they have understood well, or misunderstood, about the Christian faith.

Make some notes about how what you have read would change your approach to engaging atheists. Are there additional questions you would like to ask the writers? Clarifications you would wish to make to their understanding of Christianity? What would you ask and say if you were having a friendly chat together over coffee?

QUESTIONS

Isn't Faith in God Irrational and Outdated?

a while back I was watching a recording of two Brits on an American television network, Piers Morgan interviewing Ricky Gervais. Morgan asked Gervais how he explains his atheism to people in the US, a nation with a higher proportion of churchgoers than the United Kingdom.[1] Gervais replied that he says to Christians, "Tell me the reason that you don't believe in all the other gods, and that's the reason I don't believe in yours."

A few weeks later I attended the Oxford Union debate I mentioned in the last chapter. One of the atheist presenters, an American named Michael Shermer, gave a fifteen-minute speech against religion that culminated when he passionately told the audience, "You're all atheists for all [the] other gods, so I would just implore you to go one god further" and reject the Christian God.

My initial response was to wonder whether he had been watching the same Ricky Gervais interview as I had. But then I remembered having come across that line in a book. When I got home I grabbed the copy of Richard Dawkins's *The God Delusion* that I had borrowed from Martin Smith two years previously and had yet to return. I flipped through it and found these words:

> I have found it an amusing strategy, when asked whether I am an atheist, to point out that the questioner is also an atheist when considering Zeus, Apollo, Amon Ra, Mithras, Baal, Thor, Wotan, the Golden Calf and the Flying Spaghetti Monster. I just go one god further.[2]

So, I wondered, who was borrowing this idea from whom? Did it originate with Gervais, Shermer, Dawkins or someone else altogether?

In the end I decided that it didn't really matter. The noteworthy thing here was that one little concept—that atheism is simply a tiny step beyond disbelief in Zeus and Thor—was circulating and popping up everywhere from academic debates to television interviews and bestselling books.

I began to notice this pattern more and more. Despite the great diversity among atheists, a few key arguments and perspectives seem to recur. In this chapter we'll look at several areas that tend to be of special interest to atheists: science and religion, religious pluralism, the trustworthiness of Scripture, the plausibility of miracles, and the question of whether Christianity is simply wish fulfillment.

GOD IN A TEST TUBE: THE NATURE OF SCIENCE

Let's start with science: many atheists perceive that the findings of science are incompatible with faith in God. When I speak with atheists about God, this is often the first objection they raise to counter the plausibility of Christianity. It is therefore a topic with which we need to familiarize ourselves.

At the heart of this debate is a sense that advances in knowledge over the past two hundred years have rendered God an unnecessary hypothesis for explaining our universe. We once thought there was a designer behind the universe. But now, thanks to our discoveries of the Big Bang and Darwinian evolution, the origin and development of life can "be understood without calling upon any forces from outside the natural world—no wood sprites, no fairies, no angels, no devils, no gods or spirits of any sort," in the words of atheist physicist Victor Stenger.[3] This seems, on first glance, like a strong argument for the irrelevance of God. But it actually misunderstands both the nature of science and the definition of "God" assumed by the major religions.

We'll begin with the first of these. The philosopher Mary Midgley uses the analogy of maps to describe the relationship between science and other ways of understanding the world.[4] She points out that we can chart the same terrain in very different but nonconflicting ways. One map might show the political borders between nations, another the heights of different mountain ranges and valleys, and yet another shows the typical climate of the area. Yet they are not describing different places. Each map enables us to grasp different features of the same locations.

Midgley says the problem with writers like Dawkins is that they only acknowledge the existence of one kind of map, a physics-based one full of atoms and chemical processes. Other ways of understanding the world, such as through poetry, art, history, philosophy, literature, theology and religion, are treated as inferior and irrelevant. Our apprehension of reality becomes impoverished as a result. We need, Midgley argues, "to value and celebrate scientific knowledge without being dragged into accepting propaganda which says it is the only thing which matters."[5]

This deficiency of the science-only map to describe all reality is well illustrated in a book by Cambridge University mathematics professor John Polkinghorne. He asks his readers to imagine a boiling kettle full of water. Polkinghorne says that there are two possible explanations for why the water is bubbling up inside:[6]

1. The gas is burning, atoms are behaving differently, and the temperature is rising.

2. Somebody wants to drink a cup of tea.

The first is an answer that refers only to physical processes. It is typical of maps supplied by science. The second doesn't deny those processes but instead focuses on their ultimate cause, purpose and meaning. It resembles the map religion gives us. Both are making truth claims about the same kettle. But they are completely compatible. As Polkinghorne comments:

> We need the insights of both science and religion in our quest for understanding. Science is essentially asking, and answering, the question "How?" By what manner of means do things come about? Religion, essentially, is asking and answering the question "Why?" Is there a meaning and purpose at work behind what is happening? We need to address both these questions if we're to understand what is going on.[7]

Richard Dawkins, by contrast with Polkinghorne, admits that based on his one-map scientific perspective, "What is the purpose of the universe?" is "a silly question" with no answer. Science is simply incapable of addressing this or many other vital questions of human existence.

MORE THAN ATOMS

In C. S. Lewis's *The Voyage of the Dawn Treader,* Lucy and Eustace meet a retired star named Ramandu:

"Aren't you a star any longer?" asked Lucy.
"I am a star at rest, my daughter," answered Ramandu . . .
"In our world," said Eustace, "a star is a huge ball of flaming gas."
"Even in your world, my son, that is not what a star is but only what it is made of."[8]

Yet the maps of religion and science are not completely unrelated. It was Christian theology, in fact, that opened the door to the development of modern science. David Bentley Hart notes that the rapid "scientific, technical and theoretical accomplishments" of the last few hundred years are "largely attributable" to research undertaken in the Western university system, which was established for the teaching of Christian theology.[9] Many of the "towering figures" of early modern science were either theists (believers in one God) or Christians, including Galileo, Kepler, Pascal, Boyle, Newton, Faraday, Babbage, Mendel, Pasteur, Kelvin and Clerk Maxwell.[10] Oxford University mathematics professor John Lennox comments that their "belief in God, far from being a hindrance to their science, was often the main inspiration for it and they were not shy of saying so."[11]

That theological institutions and religious convictions should give rise to scientific research seems counterintuitive to many modern minds. Yet Christianity emphasized two key ideas that needed to be accepted before science could accelerate:

1. **God as one.** Christian thinkers, in contrast to polytheistic believers in multiple competing deities, expected unity and consistency in a universe with a single harmonious source. C. S. Lewis writes that people "became scientific because they expected Law in Nature, and they expected law in nature because they believed in a Legislator."[12]

2. **God as revealer.** Christians understood the Creator as favoring intelligible communication to his creatures. They expected anything he made, including the universe, to be accessible to human minds. Francis Bacon, a godfather of modern science, famously wrote that God has two books he gave us to read and study: Scripture and nature.[13]

The map of Christian theology, then, shaped the human imagination in such a way that the map of modern science became possible. Physicist Paul Davis, not himself a Christian, admits that "science can proceed only if the scientist adopts an essentially theological worldview . . . even the most atheistic scientist accepts as an act of faith the existence of a law-like order in nature that is at least in part comprehensible to us."[14]

Far from being at odds with one another, then, Christianity and science are longtime friends that can continue to coexist comfortably and even help each other if they don't manufacture disagreements between them or confuse their distinct emphases.

SCIENCE AND THE NATURE OF GOD

The perceived science-religion tension, though, is not only rooted in a confusion between the respective emphases of science and religion. It also stems from a misunderstanding of what Christians (and Jews and Muslims) mean by the word *God*. Many atheists assume that *God* refers to a component of our universe that can either be discovered or disproved by science. The image in many people's minds is of God as a super-powerful entity that exists *within* our universe:[15]

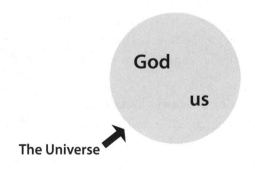

Figure 8.1

But this simply isn't how Christians understand the word *God*. They, along with Muslims and Jews, view *God* not as merely another "thing" in the universe. Instead they see him as the cause and the sustainer of reality, the one ultimately responsible for all existence. He transcends our reality, while continuing to relate to it in different ways:

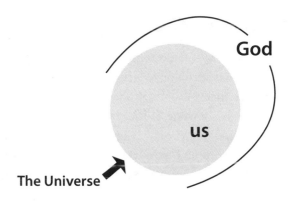

Figure 8.2

This is one reason why the "one God further" argument of Gervais and Dawkins misses the point. The concept of a single creator God causing and perhaps sustaining our reality is quite different from the idea of gods such as Thor and Baal, who were simply very special beings existing as components of our universe. You can reject "the gods" without logically needing to deny the existence of "God."

GOD OF THE GAPS

Physicist Brian Greene, an agnostic, says that the map of "science only has something to say about a very particular notion of God, which goes by the name of 'God of the gaps': if you are trying to understand the world around you and science has not yet given an explanation for some [physical] phenomenon, you could step back and say, 'Oh, that is God.' Then, when science does explain that phenomena . . . God gets squeezed out because he is no longer needed to explain that phenomena. But that is a very particular and simplistic notion of God."[16]

On this understanding of God, of course, we would expect the universe, and the sciences that measure and assess the contents of that universe, to be *consistent* with there being a creator and sustainer of all reality. But science can never hope to help us *find* or even prove God. How would it even do that? Would it produce a photograph of him on holiday in Brazil? Might someone, as Ricky Gervais has suggested, one day present "a jar of God" for laboratory testing?[17] Clearly not.

If God is going to be "found" in our world then he would need to purposefully reveal himself, to manifest himself clearly within our reality:

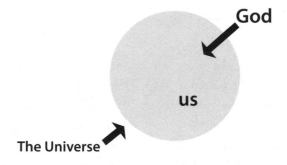

Figure 8.3

To adequately address the question of God, then, we will need to turn our attention to specific claims that he *has* revealed himself. Science might tell us the means by which the universe developed and the processes by which it ordinarily operates. But science can neither tell us why we are here nor uncover God. These are issues better addressed in other ways.

CLAIMS OF GOD

Let's suppose for a minute that God has actually revealed himself. How would we even decide which claims about God are worthy of our consideration? There seem to be so many. My atheist friend Adam told me he would love to investigate God, but it would take him years to consider all the different ideas about God.

I agreed with him that it can seem this way. But I told him that there are really only two major claims in our world that the one Creator God has shown himself. I grabbed a sheet of paper and wrote out a list of the six ways of seeing the world that are held by at least one percent of the world population, or seventy million people:[18]

- Christianity

- Islam

- agnosticism/atheism/secularism

- Hinduism

- Buddhism

- folk religions (African and Asian)

I said, "Let's eliminate those that actively deny the very existence of God." I drew a line through "agnosticism/atheism/secularism" and "Buddhism."[19] This left us with four. Then I said, "Let's get rid of those which either believe in many gods, or vaguely believe in a supreme God hovering somewhere quietly in the shadows, who has not clearly and explicitly revealed himself within human history." I crossed out "Hinduism" and "folk religions."[20]

I then drew a circle around the two remaining words, "Islam" and "Christianity." I told my friend, "This is what's left. Just two major claims in our world that there is one Creator God who has made himself known to humanity."

Adam nodded, "Thanks. That's actually really helpful. So which one do you think I should start with?"

I laughed and replied, "I think you can guess my answer to that! It's probably worth checking them both out. But you do so in slightly different ways because they each say something a bit different about how God has revealed himself. Islam views God as having spoken most clearly through a book, the Qur'an. Christianity says that God has shown himself by coming and living a human life as Jesus of Nazareth. The book matters in Christianity, but primarily because the book shows us the person. So your choice is to read the book or look at the person. What's interesting is that even the Qur'an takes Jesus seriously and describes him as a messenger of God, second only in importance to Muhammad. Looking at the person of Jesus actually lets you both investigate the core of Christianity and also a key topic of Muslims' holy book."

I pointed out to Adam that Jesus can't be investigated *scientifically* any more than Napoleon can. But he is a figure we can investigate *historically*. He's mentioned in ninety-three brief sentences in the Qur'an. These were written almost six hundred years after his death and, in most of them, his name simply forms part of a list. The Jesus story is really only told in depth in documents that stem from the decades immediately after his crucifixion. The most extensive and detailed of these are included in the New Testament and are a great staring point. Even the Qur'an agrees, telling its readers to read the "Injil," which refers to the four Gospels about Jesus.[21] This is also where I suggested to Adam that he start his investigation.

HISTORY AND JESUS

When we do turn to history, though, this doesn't mean that matters become entirely straightforward. The authenticity of the four Gospels' stories about Jesus has been challenged in numerous ways. Many critics of Christianity argue that the Gospel narratives were invented by the church long after the events they purport to record.

This perception, which is widely held, is inaccurate. Even the most *skeptical* ancient historians would not generally date the earliest Gospel, Mark, to any later than AD 70.[22] Matthew and Luke are usually not dated later than AD 90 and AD 85, respectively.[23] The *usual* dating is *at least* a decade or two earlier than this for each of the three Synoptic Gospels (as they are known). Each Gospel is commonly agreed to have drawn on preexisting (primarily oral, possibly also written) traditions, indicating that the stories they contain had been handed down for many decades previously. They overflow with the kind of authentic period detail such as "proper names, dates, cultural details, historical events, and customs and opinions of the time," which become increasingly difficult for someone to fake when they are living decades, or even centuries, later.[24] The Jesus stories in the Gospels therefore probably originated and were first spread at the very least a few years after Jesus' death. This doesn't prove beyond all doubt that the Gospels' contents are true. But it does mean that they offer an accurate glimpse into first-century perceptions of Jesus and should therefore be treated as our most valuable source for assessing him.

My friend Lucian Balanescu, an ancient historian by training, says that many dismiss the Gospels simply because they were written a long time ago. But, he points out, the measure of a historical document's value is not its chronological separation from our time period. Instead, he says we should measure its distance from the events it purports to record. He likes to sketch this diagram for people:[25]

| Jesus dies (Circa AD 30) | → | Mark written (AD 60–70) | → | Our era (21st century) |

Figure 8.4

It is the short arrow on the left that is most important. Instead of being fixated on how *old* the Gospels are, we should instead focus on how *close* their writing was to the period in which Jesus lived and died. We could even add an extra arrow to the mix and note that there isn't a very long gap between the time at which the Gospels were written and the age of the oldest surviving manuscript fragments:

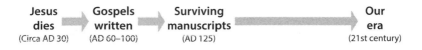

| Jesus dies (Circa AD 30) | → | Gospels written (AD 60–100) | → | Surviving manuscripts (AD 125) | → | Our era (21st century) |

Figure 8.5

The very earliest surviving biblical papyrus at the time of writing, the John Rylands Manuscript, dates from AD 125 and is a fragment of John's Gospel. We also have, dating from the late 100s and early 200s, fragments, then complete manuscripts, of most New Testament books. Though it may seem like a long gap, this is typical for all ancient documents. We virtually never possess the original scrolls, and historians are always working from later duplicates. Take, for example, the *Annals* by Tacitus, widely considered one of most important sources regarding the history of ancient Rome from the reign of Tiberius to the death of Nero. Arrows for the *Annals* would look like this:

| Nero
dies
(Circa AD 68) | *Annals*
finished
(After AD 116) | Surviving
manuscripts
(Circa AD 850) | Our
era
(21st century) |

Figure 8.6

Despite the length of the second arrow here, there is little debate as to whether the core content of this solitary AD 850 manuscript originated with Tacitus in the 100s. Similar lines could be drawn for most every major text studied by ancient historians. The New Testament stands out from all the others precisely because the second arrow—the one between its writing and the oldest extant documents—is so unusually short.

There is, then, ample evidence that the portraits of Jesus in the New Testament date from very shortly after his death and convey accurately the way he was perceived by people during the first century. Skeptics may not buy into the Gospels' contents (more on this later), but it is untenable for them to say that they are later inventions.

SUPPRESSED GOSPELS?

Another aspect of the historical discussion about Jesus is the common perception that the church suppressed a number of alternative biographies of Jesus. What we have now is sometimes said to be simply one of many competing works from the same era. When this topic arises, it's worth pointing out that the content of the New Testament was actually established by the second century at the latest. We know this for three reasons:

1. The earliest existing list of New Testament books—known as the Muratorian Fragment—dates from around AD 190. It correlates with the current content of the New Testament, as used by all sections of the church throughout history.[26]

2. Whenever the stories of Jesus are quoted in documents dating from the first few centuries of church history, the lines they cite can be found in one of our current four Gospels. Matthew, Mark, Luke and John, and not any alternative accounts, seem to have always been treated as the best eyewitness accounts of Jesus' life. Polycarp's *Letter to the Philippians* from the early 100s is typical: it quotes lines from the first three Gospels and doesn't cite any of the known extrabiblical "alternative gospels."[27]

3. The so-called other gospels are blatantly fictional accounts, and unlike the four New Testament Gospels no contemporary historian would contend they are historically reliable. Read, for example, the Gospel of Peter and you'll find the wooden cross on which Jesus died walking around and speaking to people.[28]

The early church, then, did not invent Jesus or suppress alternative accounts of his life. Even if it had wanted to do so, it possessed no power to enforce its views on anyone. For the first few centuries of its existence, the church was a heavily persecuted sect constantly fighting for its own survival.

By the time the church did first possess political and cultural power, in the late AD 300s, the New Testament documents were long established and agreed upon. Atheist journalist Matthew Parris points out that it is quite unlikely that a powerful church would invent someone so seemingly antagonistic to religion as Jesus. Parris writes:

Can you imagine the man who rode into Jerusalem on a donkey wanting anything to do with bells and smells and frocks, with gilt and silver and semi-idolatry, and repetitive chants and chorused inanities? The man who said he had come to break up families being paraded as a paradigm of family values? . . . When we consider all those painfully counterintuitive sayings and parables . . . the impatience with good works . . . it becomes ever clearer that he must have been real: if Jesus had been a hoax, the Church could have invented somebody so much more convenient.[29]

There is plenty of historical evidence that tells us that the New Testament texts accurately reflect first-century recollections of Jesus. Their reliability was recognized very early on, and there are no serious rival biographies of Jesus. When discussions about Jesus stray onto historical questions, then, we are on quite solid ground.

WONDER-WORKING MAN

Even if a person believes the New Testament dates from the first century, however, this does not mean they will accept its contents. The real reason many atheists doubt the historicity of the Gospels has nothing to do with the dating of the texts. What troubles them is the content of those manuscripts: Jesus doing miracles and rising from the dead. These things seem too much for any rational person to believe. They simply don't happen.

Atheist friends of mine often express their skepticism about the miraculous in a way that suggests they have gone through the following process:

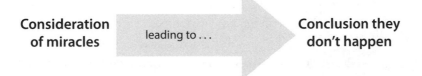

| Consideration of miracles | leading to . . . | Conclusion they don't happen |

Figure 8.7

When we talk a little more, though, it swiftly becomes apparent that most of them have actually done something more like this:

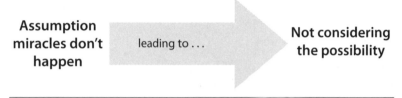

Assumption miracles don't happen — leading to ... — **Not considering the possibility**

Figure 8.8

It's therefore important to gently challenge our atheist friends to reconsider the issue with an open mind. I frequently find myself replying to doubtful questions about the miraculous by saying, "I understand your skepticism, I've shared it at times, but have you ever actually looked at the evidence? It's surprisingly strong."

This evidence relates both to Jesus' healing miracles and also to his resurrection. One thing that prevents some atheists from even considering the former is their assumption that such things were once considered normal, everyday occurrences. But this understanding of history is simply mistaken. There are few historical miracle claims that compare to those surrounding Jesus. Ancient (pre-Jesus) miracle stories were mainly about healings that occurred in the hidden confines of shrines to which visitors had to travel and in which they frequently had to sleep overnight.[30] They were generally very private and shadowy events.

A few other more well-known historical figures, such as the triangle-loving mathematician Pythagoras, had one or two strange occurrences attributed to them centuries after their deaths.[31] No one, however, had the public or prolific healing ministry attributed to Jesus. He stands out as unusual for being described as wandering from place to place, apparently healing people with regularity in broad daylight with little more than a word or a touch. These remarkable events were recorded, as we saw above, in texts dating from a few years after his death and originating from the very region where he was supposed to have healed. Even John Dominic Crossan, among the world's most skeptical scholars of the New Testament texts, admits that Jesus of Nazareth was perceived by his friends *and* enemies to be "a magician and miracle worker."[32]

THE COMEBACK KID

The most famous and controversial claim about Jesus is that he rose from the dead. This is sometimes dismissed as an "unscientific" story that nobody today could possibly believe. But this knee-jerk dismissal of the resurrection is not as common sense as it first appears: it's hardly a discovery of modern science that the dead don't return. Every culture in history has known that simple fact. Meeting a deceased loved one in the flesh would shock almost anybody who has ever lived. Yet Christianity not only *includes* but is actually *built upon* the claim that a locally famous man who was brutally murdered in public returned in full health a few days after his burial and interacted with substantial numbers of people. He even cooked breakfast for a group of them on the beach (Jn 21:9-14).

Paul's first letter to the Corinthians, near-universally agreed to have been written within two decades of Jesus' crucifixion, treats as well-worn fact that Jesus had appeared in the weeks after his murder, to more than five hundred people (1 Cor 15:3-8). Paul even names some of them. The implication is they are still alive and available to be questioned about their experiences. These sort of claims would have been as outrageous back then as they are now. In the book of Acts, in fact, audiences are recorded as sneering at the very idea of resurrection (Acts 17:32).

Yet the church grew during this period. The incredible story of the resurrection came to be accepted by large numbers of people. Many eyewitnesses to the resurrection went to their bloody deaths defending it. We have no record of anybody recanting their story, and Jesus' body was never found. His apparent resurrection was the catalyst for the launch of the world's biggest social movement and led to Jesus becoming the most famous individual in human history.

When people are skeptical about miracles, the key thing is to suggest that they look into the resurrection for themselves. Challenge them to do so with an open mind instead of deciding the issue ahead of time. Question their assumption that it *can't* happen. Suggest that they look at the evidence and decide whether it *did* happen.

"UNICORN OR SANDWICH" DILEMMA

Some atheists don't care too much for the historical arguments about the New Testament texts and their contents. For them Christianity simply seems like wish fulfilment. When I was speaking at a university recently, somebody approached me afterwards and said that he liked the idea of a loving God and the possibility of being made for a purpose. These ideas triggered something deep within him. But it just seemed too good to be true; he wondered whether Christians were simply choosing to believe something they desperately wanted to be true. Having a desire for something doesn't mean that it exists.

I sympathized. I said that I call this the "Unicorn or Sandwich" dilemma. As children, many of us were enamored with the idea of fantastical creatures like unicorns and dragons. But the fact that we wished for such things didn't mean they were real; our deepest desires don't always correlate to anything real. Perhaps our longing for God is just an adult version of wishing for unicorns. It is a beautiful fantasy that can never be realized.

He replied that this was his perspective. I then told him there was another possibility. Sometimes the very fact that we hunger for something is an indication that it actually *does* exist. Borrowing some thoughts from C. S. Lewis, I pointed out that we hunger physically because food is real, we feel sexual desire because physical intimacy is actually possible, and we want to swim because water really exists.[33] Perhaps our longing for God is not like a wish for unicorns. Perhaps it's more like being in the mood for a sandwich. Maybe our hunger correlates with something real. It's certainly interesting that, unlike a desire for unicorns, the longing for purpose in life—and also for God—carries over into adulthood and is experienced by large numbers of people.[34]

This topic of desire is an important one. At the Sunday Assembly, the atheist congregation I described in the previous chapter, the host offered a series of thoughts and anecdotes on the morning's topic of forgiveness. As he strung together a series of stories he made a throwaway remark that hit my brain like a bucket of caffeine. He said that "in evolutionary terms [forgiveness] is not what happens . . . that is why it is such a huge step to make." It stunned me because it was such a frank admission that he desires to transcend his biological origins. He, even as atheist who theoretically rejects the transcendent, feels drawn to aspire to a life that is about more than mere survival of the fittest. But is this a glitch or is it a product of living in an intrinsically moral universe?

It is here that we have an opening to move the conversation beyond issues of mere plausibility. Atheists, like everybody else, have a mixed set of feelings about the possibility of God. Some truly hope that he exists. Phil Daniels, a British actor who starred in a number of cult movies in the 1980s, was recently asked in an interview to name his greatest fear. He replied that he is most scared "that, as an atheist, I am right."[35] His sentiments echo the author Frederick Buechner's observation that the absence of God should terrify anyone who really understands the world and human nature:

> A true atheist takes human freedom very seriously. With no God to point the way, humans must find their own way. With no God to save the world, humans must save their own world if it's going to be saved. They must save it from themselves if nothing else. A true atheist does not dance on the grave of God.[36]

This is not a perspective shared by all atheists. Many conceive of atheism as a kind of freedom. Atheist philosopher Thomas Nagel frankly admits:

> I want atheism to be true and am made uneasy by the fact that some of the most intelligent and well-informed people I know are religious believers. It isn't just that I don't believe in God and, naturally, hope that I'm right in my belief. It's that I hope there is no God! I don't want there to be a God; I don't want the universe to be like that.[37]

The point here is not to tell people how they should feel or accuse them of running scared. It is a fruitless enterprise to demand someone feel a particular way about the possibility of God's nonexistence. But we can discuss these desires and fears. As we do so we may find that we move to a greater depth and honesty in our discussions.

FROM QUESTIONING TO EXPLORING

There are, then, helpful ways we can engage the major concerns and questions of our atheist friends. Most of these conversations can lead to talking about Jesus. This is not because we manipulate them that way. We just reach a point with each of these questions when we have to move from generalized discussions of a hypothetical God to grappling with the specific and widely held claim that the Creator God has made himself known in human history through the life, death and resurrection of Jesus. We find ourselves, in other words, inevitably arguing *toward* Jesus.

Atheists tend to have a broader range of criticisms against Christianity than most other groups in contemporary Western society. Perhaps this is because (unlike the other two groups discussed in the book) they are mainly affirming a negative ("I am *not* a theist") rather than a positive ("I am spiritual" or "I am Christian"). Atheists therefore need a place where they can explore their questions and also engage with the Jesus to whom so many of these questions naturally lead. The next chapter will look at some simple ways we can help them do that.

TAKING IT FURTHER

Pick one question from this chapter and write some notes about how you might adapt Luke's answers to make them appropriate for your atheist friends:

PRACTICES

Creating Safe Spaces for Exploring Questions

y experience is that most atheists enjoy the opportunity to dialogue thoughtfully about their questions. Yet Christians and atheists often both struggle to picture how this might look in practice. This problem became especially clear to me during a planning meeting for a series of small-scale events exploring the relevance of Jesus for today.

THE UNINVITED

Kay highlighted the issue for me. I'd asked everyone present whom they were thinking of bringing to the events. Kay hesitated when it came her time to speak. She said, "I would like to invite my friend Scott, but he'd cause too many problems."

My mind recalled the few times I'd met Scott. He seemed friendly and personable. I struggled to envision exactly what difficulties he would bring. Might he punch me in the face during my talk? Run around naked to distract people from the message? Arrive wearing a clown costume? The possibilities seemed endless and frequently comic. Yet none fitted with what I'd seen of Scott.

So I asked, "Really, what problems would he cause?"

"Oh," Kay replied, "he's an atheist and says he has so many objections to Christianity that we just wouldn't want him there. And I agree; he'd probably just ask something awkward."

I'd love to tell you this was the first time this conversation had occurred. But it happens frequently in different forms. Kindly and sensitive atheists avoid coming near the church for fear that they may ruin our party if they fully articulate their thoughts about the implausibility of Christianity. They worry that the fragile balloon of our faith may pop when it comes into contact with the sharp edge of their criticisms.

Christians can often compound this situation. They just can't imagine situations in which their atheist friends' questions are being engaged thoughtfully. Perhaps they lack confidence that their beliefs can withstand hard questions. Mostly, though, I think they have few models of good practice in this area.

When Kay told me about Scott's skepticism, I said, "Wow, he actually sounds like exactly the kind of guy we'd love to have along. Tell him we only want him to be there if he's ready to ask his hardest and best questions."

I wasn't being hubristic. If Scott would just come I was sure he would find a place where his perspective was taken seriously. He would also, I hoped, have an opportunity to grapple with the best case for Jesus. My confidence lay partly in practices I have learned, whether in person or through books, from three people: Stefan Gustavsson, Michael Green and Dan Kimball. Perhaps as you meet them now, their experiences and perspectives will help you too. Let's start with a visit to a potentially tense situation that turned out to be unexpectedly cordial.

MICRO PRACTICE: CONVERSATION FLIPPING

One reason for the tension was the numbers at the university Philosophy Society. Nineteen atheists and three Christians. To my left in the circle of chairs sat a Swede named Stefan Gustavsson. I'd first met him five years previously at a training event in Hungary and had been impressed by his insistence that we stop referring to people outside the church as "unbelievers." *Everybody*, he explained, believes *something*, and through asking good questions we can uncover those core convictions and explore their validity. So, when the opportunity eventually arose, I sent him an email and asked whether he would come and spend a few days interacting with students on university campuses in my area of the United Kingdom.

I was eager to see how he would operate in such an intimidating setting. We were on the atheists' turf, and many of their eyes displayed a glint normally reserved for hungry Roman lions. It was everything Scott might have expected from an encounter between Christians and atheists. It looked like Stefan's only alternative to being eaten alive in this modern-day coliseum would be to bite back. And hard.

But it didn't happen that way. By the time the meeting ended two hours later, we were all—Christian and atheist alike—walking out together smiling and happy. Not because any of us had defeated our mighty foes. Nor because we had avoided the topic of God and retreated to less contested ground. Our shared joy came from the fact that we had been able to openly and thoughtfully engage with one another's perspectives.

The first question, following Stefan's introductory twenty-minute talk on the existence of God, had been hostile and dismissive. But Stefan hadn't punched back. Instead he warmly affirmed the questioner, gave a brief two-minute reply, and then gently invited the questioner to respond and give his thoughts on the topic. A potentially heated argument had been converted into a respectful and friendly dialogue.

The whole event made a lasting impression on me. Stefan seemed to decisively win the key arguments, yet everybody still liked him. At the heart of this outcome was his ability to convert potentially fractious encounters into warm, two-way explorations of life's big questions.

Stefan and I were most recently together in Prague, at a gathering of university evangelists from around Europe, and I asked him how he had first begun to have these kinds of conversations. He replied by telling me about his upbringing. He grew up in the most secularized corner of Sweden and was the only churched teenager in his entire school. There was never any possibility of him preaching or imposing his ideas on others. The sole possible route to speaking about Jesus was by learning to ask good questions and challenge others conversationally.

Lots of Christians struggle, Stefan said, to have constructive conversations about Jesus with atheists and others who are not his followers. The main model of communication in the church tends to be the monologue. Sermons and presentations dominate. Yet when we flick through the pages of the four Gospels we find Jesus far from dependent on one-way communication. Most of the time he is interacting on a personal level with individuals and groups.

One friend of mine, Nasrin, says that Stefan's conversational approach was key to her beginning to follow Jesus. Nasrin was bisexual, atheist and a radical feminist when she first met Stefan. She somehow managed to get herself enrolled in Credo Academy, the apologetics training school he runs in Stockholm, and made no attempt to disguise her skepticism or the breadth of objections she held toward Christianity. Yet she says Stefan always responded with warmth and kindness. He took all her questions seriously and listened well. He gently gave convincing answers to her concerns and "always left me with a new set of questions to ponder." Over the first year she knew him, she moved from hostility and unbelief to passionately following Jesus for herself. Today she is married to another Jesus follower and is raising their four children to themselves love and know God.

Stefan, in his interactions at the philosophy society and with Nasrin, offers a great model for engaging those around us, epecially atheists, who have substantial objections to the Christian faith. Like Stefan among his unchurched schoolmates, we often find ourselves powerless with conversation as the only possible way forward. There are no pulpits in most workplaces, friendships and families. We should therefore avoid our natural temptation to preach at others and instead develop the skill of exploring life's big questions through friendly conversational interactions.

IT TAKES TIME

Virtually everybody who begins following Jesus does so partly because of a friendship with a Christian. Doug Schaupp and Don Everts interviewed hundreds of Jesus' followers about their spiritual journeys for their book *I Once Was Lost.*[1] They found that almost every single interviewee had passed through the same five stages on their way to knowing God. These "thresholds . . . of conversion" are, in order:

1. Trusting a Christian

2. Becoming Curious

3. Opening Up to Change

4. Seeking After God

5. Entering the Kingdom

Trusting a Christian is therefore invariably the first step towards following Jesus. I have known people to pass through all five phases in a couple of hours. Ordinarily, though, it seems to take at least six months. Stefan's low-key conversational approach is critical in such long-term relational settings.

I asked Stefan what advice he would give someone looking to emulate, in their own settings, the kind of cordial dialogues I saw modeled at the university Philosophy Society. Stefan said he couldn't put it better than the Greek philosopher Aristotle, who emphasized "ethos, pathos and logos." He broke down these three elements for me as follows:

- **Ethos** is all about you as a person. Are you credible? In some settings this has to do with academic qualifications or others' recognition of your expertise. But that's unlikely to be the priority with most people you meet. They will instead judge your credibility on a wider range of criteria. They will ask if you take their questions seriously. Are you a good listener? It matters whether you work hard to understand them before you strive to make yourself understood. You will also need to exude grace and patience. An argumentative and arrogant person is rarely deemed credible. We simply cannot press pause on being Christlike and respectful as soon as we start interacting with the questions and objections of atheists.

- **Pathos** is the emotional element. You'll need to appeal to more than reason. Stefan says that he likes to prod the imagination. He told me that his approach is often "suggestive"; he asks questions such as, "You'd agree it's possible there's a God . . . I'm not saying there is, but it's possible, don't you think?" Few people would contest the slim possibility of God's existence. Then Stefan might say, "If it's possible God exists, then what if he wants to make himself known to us? How might he do that?" Stefan told me that this is "not a technique." He has no pre-prepared set of questions he uses. He just wants people to admit the possibility of God and then begin imagining what it might mean if he did exist. Stefan compared asking such questions to making small snowballs and rolling them down a snowy hill. Soon, as our conversation partners begin pondering them, the possibilities of God begin gaining momentum and weight entirely on their own.

- **Logos** is the aspect of our interactions that has to do with reasoned argumentation. It's about plausibility. Those who value truth and consider themselves rational tend to find their sense of Christianity's desirability and tangibility accentuated by its plausibility. The three are intertwined. We therefore desperately need to be able to address atheists' most pressing questions and gently argue a strong case for Jesus. The key to this, Stefan told me, is the capacity to simplify. We need to understand the main issues under debate well enough to succinctly convey our perspective in a conversational setting. This requires some work. We'll need to discern the most common objections we encounter to Christianity, then read and listen to the best responses we can find to these questions.

I was reminded, as Stefan spoke to me about logos, of a story our mutual friend Lindsay Brown often tells. When Lindsay was twenty-two years old he made a list of the eleven most common questions his non-church friends posed to him. Then, for a year and with the advice of mentors, he spent much of his spare time working through the list and figuring out how to answer them. Now, four decades later, he says those months of research continue to underpin a ministry that has allowed him to speak about Jesus in more than one hundred different countries.

Chapters five, eight and eleven (labeled "Questions") of this book are designed to give you a head start on this process by outlining some key arguments. Perhaps your next step could be to pick the one question from this book that you find most frequently occurs in conversation with others. Then begin investigating it further. Select a book on that topic (see appendix three for some suggestions), and order it so it arrives in time to start right after you finish this one.

Stefan's model of gently converting questions into conversations is one we can all imitate even with the knowledge and understanding we have right now. Pathos, ethos and even a bit of logos are within the grasp of almost any Christian. We'll all obviously want to develop further in all three areas. But you can *begin* exercising them the very next time you converse with an atheist.

MESO PRACTICE: AGNOSTICS ANONYMOUS

Conversations around big questions don't need to be restricted to spontaneous moments. Michael Green, a friend and mentor of mine, recently told me a story about when he was first pastoring in a large university city. Most of the students at his church lived in shared accommodation. They were surrounded by people who weren't Christians, and their faith naturally became an occasional topic of discussion. Michael suggested to the students that they ask their friends, "Why don't you let me and another Christian cook you dinner, and you can all tell us why you don't believe, and maybe we can tell you why we do?"

Five students came to the first such event. As they spoke together Michael jotted down a list of the students' stated objections to Christianity. Some were familiar to him, while others were unexpected. At the end of the evening, Michael read the list aloud to everyone. He asked, "Why don't we meet each week and talk together about one of these topics?" Everybody thought it was a great idea, and so began a weekly gathering that led to several of them becoming followers of Jesus.

It's now more than forty years later, and Michael continues to host similar low-key gatherings over food. He refers to them as Agnostics Anonymous meetings. He's personally seen numerous people come to a lasting faith in Christ through such get-togethers. While many evangelistic methodologies have come and gone, Michael told me, this very simple approach is one that can still be successfully adapted for a range of contexts.

The basic template for an Agnostics Anonymous gathering runs in this order:

1. Begin with informal mingling and conversation.

2. Serve food.

3. The host outlines the purpose: to share reasons why we don't believe (in God) or reasons why we do.

4. Over dinner, guests share why they don't believe.

5. The host gives a short minitalk of less than ten minutes, referencing what has been shared and also offering reasons why he/she does believe.

6. The host suggests some next steps for people who want to continue exploring these topics.

7. The group engages in more informal mingling and conversation.

Michael sometimes still uses this approach with university students. He also employed it during his two years of helping plant a church in North Carolina and saw around a hundred new Christians—mainly families—come to faith through such discussions. Even now, in their eighties, Michael and his wife continue to do something similar with those over fifty years old in the local area. Most of those attending over the past two years have come to faith.

I asked Michael why he thought this approach still works so well. From stories I hear from Michael and others, it seems that it's more effective today than ever. Michael replied that we live in a non-authoritarian culture. Many people are quite resistant to being told what they should think. Sharing meals together levels relationships and opens everyone to engaging more openly with the topics being discussed. Since people enjoy these kinds of conversations it's very easy to convert such one-off events into an ongoing seeking community. It also only requires equipment you likely already possess: a place to meet with a kitchen.

My friend Kip, a Kenyan who lives in Britain, recently told me that he'd been reading through the Gospel of Luke and noticed that almost every scene features Jesus eating, going *from* a meal or walking *to* a dinner table somewhere. He said that most Westerners probably completely filter out the "meal-centric" nature of Jesus' ministry when reading these stories. We joked together about why no painters or filmmakers ever portray Jesus as portly. He certainly ate frequently enough to risk carrying some extra weight. Perhaps all the walking in between helped him stay trim.

It's pretty straightforward to host an Agnostics Anonymous meeting for yourself. As we sat in the sunshine together a couple of weeks ago sipping coffee, I asked Michael what tips he'd give to someone wanting to run their own such discussion. He gave me these six pointers:

- **Start with a group of people with whom you are already in relationship.** Between two and twelve is the ideal number. Tell your friends that a group of you, mostly agnostic and undecided about religion, will be getting together to eat and also to chat about why they don't believe and why you do. Make sure that a minority of those present are already Christians. Ideally you should have no more than two Jesus followers present. This makes the airing of questions much easier and keeps newcomers from feeling like a beleaguered minority.

- **Plan the evening ahead of time.** Take time to think about how you will smoothly transition from the initial unstructured conversations to a more focused discussion around the evening's topic. Consider how to pitch your tone and manner so that they are natural and low-key. Craft your discussion-starting questions and your minitalk so that they open up good conversations rather than shut them down.

- **Serve excellent food.** Demonstrate good hospitality and give your guests the best meal you can make (or buy). It will show that you value them and also makes for a more enjoyable and relaxed evening.

- **Allow your friends to help shape the agenda for discussion.** Go around the group and have everyone share why they do or don't believe. Make it a safe place where people can share their own stories of doubts, questions and unbelief. Take brief notes of people's responses and let the concerns of those present inform future discussions. Be prepared to recalibrate your minitalk so it makes reference to things that have been said.

- **Maintain a focus on Jesus.** In his minitalks, Michael makes a very basic introduction to Jesus and his message. He also often says toward the end of these gatherings, "This has been a great discussion . . . if you really want to think more seriously about these issues, though, the heart of Christianity is Christ. What if we get together again next week and go back to the original texts which tell his story, then discuss our thoughts and reactions to them?" People often like the idea of going back to the original documents and using the source materials to assess Jesus.

- **Close your time together with a challenge.** Too often we have discussions with people that end with a suggestion to think about what's been said. Michael says we need to invite people to take action: come back the following week, read a short booklet and discuss it, or something similar. To do this, you will have to have a follow-up event already planned. Ask everyone to pull out their phones or calendars and schedule the next get-together before anyone goes home.

It's very easy to replicate and also adapt Michael's approach. Last year, when I was assisting Michael in a week of events run by a local church, members of the congregation opened their homes to neighbors and friends for events such as whiskey tasting and a chocolate dessert evening. Each one was patterned according to some variation of the Agnostics Anonymous template. Kip, my Kenyan friend, pointed out to me that "the Son of Man came eating and drinking" (Mt 11:19). Agnostics Anonymous is one way to follow his example.

BE FLEXIBLE

Your get-togethers could be for a defined period ("the next three weeks") or they could be more occasional and built around participants' schedules and availability (a great online tool for matching schedules is Doodle.com). You could also rotate the hosting and meal preparation; some people feel safer on their own home turf. Michael's model is endlessly adaptable for different settings and people.

MACRO PRACTICE: SAFE SPACES

One of the reasons Agnostics Anonymous works is because it offers a protected space in which people feel free to share what they really think. Disagreement and objections are expected and welcomed. This sense of safety and freedom doesn't have to be restricted to small, home-based gatherings. It can also become a feature of the larger gatherings of your church. Dan Kimball, author of the excellent *They Like Jesus but Not the Church*, believes one of the keys to engaging contemporary people and especially atheists with the story of Jesus is to transform the entire church into one big safe space.

Vintage Faith Church, the community he leads in Santa Cruz, California, sees a steady stream of people come to faith from atheistic backgrounds. When Dan and I recently spoke on Skype he walked around with his laptop and took me on a tour of his church building, introducing me to different people with whom he conducted impromptu interviews.

One young woman we met described to me how she had become open to Jesus because she felt such a freedom to be honest about her own doubts and questions. She'd been invited by a friend to visit The Abbey, the church's coffee shop. Intrigued by the artwork on the walls, she soon found herself making a scouting trip to a Sunday service. There, despite her atheist background, she had her preconceptions about Jesus and Christians challenged.

Dan asked, "You must have had some tough questions when you first came. Where did you go with them?" She shrugged and smiled. "Yeah, I still have loads of questions," she said matter-of-factly, "but I just ask anybody in the church; everybody is happy to listen and help." She clearly felt at ease to be herself and had a sense that the whole church was a place where she could be open about aspects of Christianity she finds hard to believe.

I asked Dan why it was important to him that the church have such a welcoming attitude toward the questions of people like this young woman. He replied that when he first began following Jesus as a twenty-something rock drummer most of his friends and family were not Christians. They would fire great questions and objections at him about his newfound faith. He didn't want to give them superficial or unsatisfactory answers, so he worked hard at listening well to what they said and then researched the most helpful responses he could find. When he later found his way into Christian ministry, he continued this habit of treating objections to Christianity seriously, and this quality defined the communities he led.

The key to Vintage Faith's success seems to be that space for questions is not simply an appendage to an otherwise close-minded and preachy church culture. Members and visitors are constantly encouraged to be open about the areas where they struggle to find Christianity either plausible or desirable. Difficult questions are welcomed and there is a sense that nobody has to pretend to understand or agree with everything they hear. But they do have the chance to grapple with the best available responses to their concerns. It's a compelling blend of confidence in the truth and unpressured freedom to explore.

I asked Dan how a church can develop a similarly open-yet-confident internal culture. He replied that it "all starts with the church's leadership." If a church's leaders are passionate about inviting new people to begin following Jesus, then it will be very natural for them to embrace people who arrive with a big bag of misgivings toward Christianity. They'll constantly be looking for ways to reassure newcomers that doubts are normal, and even the trickiest questions are welcomed. One of the things I noticed about Dan's interactions with people in the church is that everyone seems relaxed and speaks naturally with him. This sets the tone for the whole church. Most people at Vintage Faith actually work through their questions in the informal context of interpersonal relationships. But Dan cautioned, "If your leadership team is not enthusiastic about evangelism, this will need to change before your church can become a safe space."

Assuming a church has a passionate leadership, the next step is to "rethink every major component of your ministry." Dan gave me three examples of how his church does this:

1. Vintage Faith Church's building is designed to invite engagement and not just spectatorship. It is full of art created locally. This is a way of "inviting people to interact and not just consume." Vintage Faith Church also decided that, instead of pouring their money into a fancy Sunday worship venue, they would invest in developing an excellent coffee shop for locals. The Abbey has twice been voted the best student hangout in Santa Cruz. All these are small ways in which church life is constructed as collaborative rather than simply consumeristic. Interaction and engagement feel natural in such a setting.

2. Dan and the teaching team intentionally include apologetic elements in their Sunday Bible teaching. For example, when Dan recently spoke about Philip's encounter with the Ethiopian man in Acts 8, he told the congregation a story about a conversation with his barber. With his barber's permission, he recalled many of his hairdresser's questions and shared some of his own answers. Dan's sermon wasn't specifically about addressing difficulties with Christianity. It was actually a challenge to follow the Holy Spirit's leading to engagement with specific individuals. But through his story about the barber he modeled good conversational practice. Dan says that this is his normal mode of operation; he demonstrates apologetics through his stories. He also deals with hot topics and potential objections whenever they arise within the texts and topics upon which he is teaching.

3. Vintage Faith Church does more than simply preemptively address questions that may be on everyone's minds. They also create opportunities for people to publicly air their questions and engage them. Sunday sermons on controversial and difficult topics, for example, are usually followed the next night by something called "Open Forum." This is a time when people can come and ask their

questions or discuss their ideas with the previous day's speaker. People can also submit questions anonymously if they prefer, in writing or even by texting. This can work really well if you have the right person answering the questions from the front. Dan says these open forums do more than just help address individuals' difficulties. They also help create a tone that says "it's OK not to be sure or to have lots of doubts."

Cultivating a sense of openness towards newcomers and their questions, then, is not something a church can achieve in one easy move. It requires that an evangelistically passionate leadership team begin carefully rethinking each aspect of the community's life together. But doing so will reap great rewards. Atheists, not to mention the Christians, will appreciate the shift in tone.

YOUR ATHEIST FRIENDS

Kay's friend Scott would have benefitted from any of these three practices. Having his questions converted into conversations, exploring reasons for belief and unbelief over a delicious dinner, or encountering a community that was a safe space for honest discussion would each have helped him begin thinking clearly about Jesus.

The good news is that some of those things did happen. Kay ended up inviting Scott to the first in our series of events, a variation on the Agnostics Anonymous template. It was a pleasant surprise for him to discover that tough questions were invited and that the Christians present were able to thoughtfully make the case for Jesus. The capacity of Christianity to withstand the battering of his tough criticisms forced him to reconsider his previous dismissal of it as an option for his life.

I last saw Scott six months after Kay first told me she wouldn't invite him to our events. He had become an occasional attendee at Christian gatherings and was developing some good friendships with a range of Jesus' followers. He wasn't yet convinced. But he was open and taking Jesus seriously for the first time in his life. Perhaps one of these practices can help your atheist friends do the same thing. Not everyone who doesn't believe in God will be as unbending and hard-hearted as Richard Dawkins, and many would love to discover an environment where they can put their convictions to the test.

TAKING IT FURTHER

Do you think your atheist friends are reticent to criticize Christianity in your presence or keen to do so?

If they are reticent, what could you do to help them feel that they won't offend you and that their questions are welcome? Pause to reflect on this, and note some possible next steps:

Alternatively, if your friends are keen to criticize, might it be possible to parlay that willingness to talk into a series of Stefan-style conversations between the two of you? Pause to reflect on this, and note some possible next steps:

STORIES

The Pimp, the Planter and Their Friends

THE PIMP AND THE PLANTER

"Do you want a girl?"

The taxi driver's words took me by surprise. "A girl?" I asked, wondering whether this man moonlit as a dating agent. "Like a girlfriend?"

"No," he smiled with a twinkle in his eye. "A working girl, a girl for the night, I can find you a good price."

I paused for a moment, and then asked naively, "Do you mean a prostitute?"

"Yes, I find you a good price, I take lots of people there," he replied, before proceeding to quote me some possible costs.

I cut him off mid-sentence. "No, I'm really fine, thanks, I'm not interested."

He seemed confused and asked, "Why not?"

"Well . . ." I began, "I'm a Christian, and . . ."

It was now his turn to stop me mid-flow.

"Christian?!" he bellowed with a hint of dismissive laughter. "I am Christian, look . . ."

He waved his arms around the cab. I saw that his dashboard was plastered with glittering icons, mainly of Jesus and Mary. The rear view mirror doubled as a peg to hang rosaries and crosses. He reached down inside his shirt and pulled a silver crucifix out to show me.

"Christian," he repeated. "I am Christian, you are Christian, we are all Christian, but we are also men. And we cannot let our religion tell us how we live."

This kind of conversation would have been unimaginable to me a few years ago. For my first few years of high school I was the only kid in my grade who went to church. Nobody else even openly called themselves Christian. It was a huge surprise, then, when I discovered that most Western people, even in my supposedly irreligious homeland of Britain, tick "Christian" on any form that asks for their religion. In my schoolboy mind a Christian was a committed, regular churchgoer whose life reflected the teachings of Jesus. The idea that somebody might offer me sex for money while wearing a crucifix was quite inconceivable.

If I had to imagine the model Christian, I would probably think of Dave. We first met when he was part of a group of students planting a new Christian community on a previously unreached university campus. Dave had grown up in a committed Baptist family and had a good handle on the basics of the faith. He was a faithful friend to others, steadfast in his sexual purity and unusually sober for someone studying at a campus renowned for its extreme drinking culture. Other Christian students trusted him easily, and he was soon offered the leadership of this newly planted group.

Dave and I collaborated for two years in pioneering the work among his fellow students. We eventually parted ways when I left full-time campus ministry to pursue further theological study. Dave also moved away to spend a year gaining work experience in his planned career of vehicle design. We didn't expect to see each other for a while.

Six months after saying farewell, though, he was sitting next to me on a couch, staring blankly at the floor. He seemed traumatized and had tears in his eyes. We'd unexpectedly reconnected when I was speaking at a retreat co-run by the group we'd helped start. I'd just given the Saturday night talk on what it means to be born again and had invited those who wanted to respond to come and pray with someone in the adjoining room.

So, that's where we were, sitting in silence: the prayer room. Dave had been the first person through the door. Finally, after a few minutes, Dave slowly looked up at me, took a deep breath to steady himself, and said, "I'm not a Christian, Luke. I never have been, and I've probably always known it."

Dave later told me that he'd connected with the pioneering university work as a student because he'd been raised to think that Christian community is "what you do." He'd been surprised to so rapidly find himself in a leadership position but was happy to help out. He enjoyed his role. But whenever people prayed or spoke about their relationship with God he simply couldn't relate. Lurking in the back of his mind was a sense that he shouldn't just know about God. He should experience him. When he left university to work in vehicle design his church attendance became sporadic. It slowly dawned on him that when community was removed, so was his entire Christian experience—there was simply no personal connection between him and God.

As I spoke at the retreat he had become completely conscious of God's absence in his life. He was suddenly consumed by a sense of his need for Jesus. After his confession on the sofa we sat in more silence as I absorbed his words and silently prayed for direction about what to say next.

In the end I simply asked, "So, would you like to make the kind of response I described tonight?" Dave nodded and said, "Yes," and we closed our eyes as he prayed a heartfelt prayer asking for forgiveness and giving his life over to God. His words were halting and raw, possessed with an unpolished authenticity that had never been a feature of his previous prayers.

I then prayed for Dave. Then I told him that I sensed that God saw him as the prodigal son coming home and that maybe, on his behalf, God wanted me to hug him as a physical mark of the Father's welcome. As British males neither of us really do physical contact outside the family and playing sports. But it was a beautiful moment of being able to tangibly embody God's joyful embrace of Dave. Even now, several years later, he still sees these moments as the start of knowing God for himself.

Dave *seems* like a very different character to the sex-selling taxi driver. But they both considered themselves to be Christians. So did my schoolmates who knew virtually nothing about Jesus but still ticked "Christian" on their census forms. In reality, however, none of them had encountered Christ, nor had they opened their lives up to him.

More Than a Name

Dave and the taxi driver were both nominal Christians when I first met them, meaning that they bore the name of Jesus but were not his followers. It would be easy to label them both as hypocrites and to dismiss their Christian professions as simply a mask to cover their true nature. But this is not an accurate assessment of either individual. They were both quite sincere about their religion. It meant something to them, enough to expend great energy on planting a new Christian community in Dave's case; sufficient to plaster the dashboard with paintings of Jesus and his mom in the taxi driver's case. Dave and the taxi driver were certainly missing something quite vital. But they were not fakes.

Neither were they burnt out and cynical about church. Dave was a lifelong, committed Baptist. The taxi driver openly identified with his own denomination of Eastern Orthodoxy. My subsequent conversation with him, though, revealed that he rarely attended church. He would be there at Christmas, Easter and times of crisis. The rest of the time he was happy to spend his Sunday mornings with his children.

Protestants and especially evangelicals often find it hard to understand that people can have such a casual relationship with their church and still self-identify as members of their denomination. Eddie Gibbs says that this is partly because evangelicals usually conceive of church as the "gathered" people of God.[1] For them, being part of a church is largely defined by regularly showing their face at the meetings of a local Christian community. They usually equate nonattendance with disinterest or backsliding.

Roman Catholicism and Eastern Orthodoxy also value and encourage local church involvement. But their conception of church often has a slightly different emphasis. Baptism, usually in infancy, tends to constitute a more meaningful marker of belonging than Sunday attendance. Many Catholic and Eastern Orthodox leaders "consider their nonactive constituency not as unbelievers in need of evangelizing, but as vulnerable Christians with a fragile faith, in need of pastoral care."[2] Occasional church involvement, then, is not usually perceived by priests—or by ordinary members—as a rejection of their religion. There is therefore often no felt contradiction between fiercely affirming one's personal Christian commitment and also having little ongoing connection with a local church. This is especially true in settings such as Polish Catholicism or Greek Orthodoxy, in which Christian identity is closely tied to cultural or ethnic backgrounds. It tends to be less the case among some of the newer Orthodox churches in the United States, which are largely constituted of newer converts who joined the denomination by choice in adulthood.

This is not to say that there aren't Protestant or evangelical equivalents of my taxi driver, people who happily identify with the church yet have a limited active relationship with it. This is most common in places where Christianity still holds an honored place in the cultural mainstream. The Bible Belt is one such place. My wife, Whitney, a native South Carolinian, says that growing up she barely knew anyone who couldn't name their denominational identity. But a relatively smaller number of her acquaintances actually followed Jesus or even regularly attended church. This particular kind of nominalism has cultural, rather than theological, roots. But its outcome is very similar to Catholic and Eastern Orthodox nominalism.

Church attendance, then, should not be taken as a measure of a given person's attitude to Christ or to the church. The taxi driver and Dave each had a high regard for both. I was surprised when the former told me he was a Christian. But I did not point my finger back at him and say he was not a real believer. Instead I asked him what his Christianity meant to him and inquired about his relationship with God. His self-identification as Christian offered an excellent opportunity for us to spend the latter part of our journey discussing Jesus rather than arguing about the authenticity of his faith profession.

THE WANDERERS

Not every nominal Christian identifies as readily with the church as Dave and the taxi driver. Some have had extensive past involvement with a local congregation but have since stepped away. They still bear the name Christian but are estranged from the church and not sure they actually believe many of Christianity's most basic tenets.

James is just such a person. Having grown up in a Christian family, he was fully involved in the youth group at his local Methodist church and was raised with Bible stories every night before bed. During his teens, though, he began to have some big questions and doubts about what was being taught in church. Questions about science were troubling to him. So were various doctrines, such as hell, that he found difficult to swallow.

His parents weren't really able to answer his questions satisfactorily. He trusted the youth pastor, however, and began to discuss some of his concerns with him. They began meeting together every week to chat over coffee. After a couple of months, though, the youth pastor was fired after experiencing a falling out with the senior minister. There began to be rumblings of a split in the church, and the atmosphere turned frosty. James began to withdraw emotionally from the church community.

When a new youth pastor was appointed his hopes were raised afresh. James thought this might be a chance to begin working through his doubts again. They met together, and James fired a series of his questions at him. The new youth pastor said that James was overthinking these things and that he should really just have a little faith. This hardened James's sense that there may not be good answers to his questions. Perhaps church was not for people who want to raise awkward topics. When he went to university a year later he never connected with a church or campus group. He found his ethical outlet through groups such as Amnesty International.[3] By the time he graduated he had abandoned all but the moral teachings of orthodox Christianity.

James's story is far from unique. Research suggests that as many as 80 percent of American teenagers have some kind of association with a church during their teenage years.[4] Many of these are the children of believing parents. Others are from nonreligious families and are invited to youth groups or camps by churched friends. Not all these teenagers make a clear Christian commitment during this time, but many will do so. By the time they reach their early twenties, however, barely 40 percent of them will still be in church.[5] That's an incredible drop off in a very short period of time.

For the children of unchurched families this departure may not have been very painful. They may look back warmly on their teenage church involvement as a fun activity and move on to other nonreligious activities during their twenties. Their adolescent church connection may even make them more open to considering Jesus afresh when they get to know other Christians later in life.

But for those from Christian families, and also for others who made some kind of sincere commitment during their formative years, leaving the church may be a more mixed experience. Interviews with people who have left the faith suggest that they generally don't abandon Christianity by accident. They tend to do so for at least one of the following three reasons:

- disagreement with specific Christian teachings
- discomfort with the culture of the church
- bad experiences with other Christians[6]

Any interaction with a "former Christian," then, is an engagement with somebody who has a complex backstory underlying their drift from the church. Author and scholar Scot McKnight notes that many of "those who leave the faith feel like jilted lovers or even betrayed by the one they loved."[7] We will need to listen carefully to their experiences to grasp exactly what led them to their current situation.

Sensitive family situations are often a part of these stories. Academic studies show that the children of Christian parents *normally* become followers of Jesus. The Longitudinal Study of Generations, an incredible sociological project that has interviewed and tracked four generations of more than 350 families over the past few decades, has found that there are only three circumstances in which it is more probable a person will reject their parents' Christianity rather than embrace it.[8] These situations are:

- They have a distant relationship with their father.
- Their parents are divorced.
- Their parents are from two different religions.[9]

The first two of these are ordinarily quite painful experiences. The third can *sometimes* also create conflict within the home. We should therefore be aware, in our interactions with friends who have rejected Christianity, that there may be a difficult set of family relationships that have played a part in their alienation from the faith. They may be as much pushing away from their parents and upbringing as they are from Jesus.

This is not always the case. I know several people from warm and stable families who have rejected the Christianity of their parents. But difficult family dynamics feature in many journeys away from the Christian faith. We therefore need to constantly remind ourselves that we are interacting with people and their life stories and not just with ideas.

(Un)true Believers?

One of the most common questions about seemingly nominal individuals is whether or not they are genuinely Christian. Are they "in" or "out"? This difficulty becomes especially apparent when we consider each of the four major groupings of nominal Christians highlighted so far in this chapter:

Table 10.1. Categories of Nominal Christians

	Churched	Casual	Wanderer	Official
Relationship with church	regular and committed	occasional; mainly festivals	past involvement, present estrangement	none, except perhaps baptism
Attitude to church	usually positive	usually positive or indifferent	usually negative or indifferent	could be anything
Beliefs	essentially Christian	elements of Christianity	elements of Christianity	could be anything
Example in this chapter	Dave, the pious campus leader	the pimping taxi driver	James, the doubting Methodist	otherwise secular Brits who check "Christian" on forms

"Official" Christians are the simplest category to assess. They are almost always followers of Jesus in name only. They simply have not had enough contact with the church to have ever developed an accurate understanding of Jesus or to have made any response to him. We can generally assume they are not Christian in any substantial sense of the word.

"Wanderers" are another group that includes clearly unconverted individuals. But many wanderers have not permanently abandoned the faith. They may have drifted from involvement with a local church and might also be grappling with unresolved questions. But they have not necessarily stopped believing. J. R. R. Tolkien observes in *The*

Lord of the Rings that "not all those who wander are lost," and this certainly applies to the many Christians who have periods when they slip out of active church involvement or find themselves passing through a temporary phase of doubt only to come out the other side much stronger.[10] Such undulations in personal commitment and belief are part of numerous healthy spiritual journeys that end up lasting a lifetime.

Churched and casual nominals are also tough to gauge. Dave, the student leader, looked like a passionate Christian to all who met him. No one knew what was going on inside. Other, more casual members of Dave's campus group during the same period seemed less clearly Christian. Over the years that followed, however, their simple and fragile faith grew into something lasting and strong. Appearances can be deceptive and often time reveals what is really going on.

One of the reasons we find this question of "in or out" so difficult is that we are accustomed to thinking of Christian conversion as something that always occurs at a single moment in time. There was a preacher I once knew who would tell everybody that if they couldn't name the exact day they turned to Christ then their conversion was not real. People in his congregation all ended up either making a new "decision for Christ" just to be sure, or they arbitrarily selected a significant day from their own spiritual history and designated that as the day of their conversion.

Interestingly, though, the New Testament doesn't portray conversion as always being instantaneous. Take Jesus' close friend Peter as an example. Try reading the Gospels and figuring out when Peter was converted. Was it when he started following Jesus? When he realized Jesus was the Messiah? When he was sent out to preach and heal? When Jesus forgave him for denying him? It's just not that clear-cut.[11]

Even Billy Graham, who was famed for calling people forward after he preached so that they could make "a decision for Christ," never labeled these important spiritual moments as "conversions." This probably stemmed from his life experience. John Stackhouse points out that "according to [Billy Graham's] several biographers and his own memoirs, Billy Graham has experienced what amount to three, and perhaps four, major spiritual turning points in his life. More than one of them some might call conversion experiences."[12]

Some people do seem to have near-instantaneous conversions. You probably know some of them. But such experiences are by no means universal. Conversion is a process. Most people will experience several pivotal spiritual moments. Knowing this can help us shift our engagement with apparently nominal Christians from a simplistic question of "are they in or out?" to a more nuanced one of "where are they in the process?"

RETHINKING CONVERSION

Asking such a question, though, requires that we understand a little more about how conversion works. In his excellent book *Beginning Well*, Gordon Smith describes conversion as the "response" people make "to the invitation, love, and work of God in Christ."[13] It might be a very quick response, or it might occur over a longer period of time, but it is all about how people respond to Jesus.

This means that nominal Christians, like all other people, need to engage with Jesus and not simply with a new, improved version of church. A full response to Jesus, according to Smith, includes "a cluster of seven distinct elements."[14] These seven elements don't necessarily occur in the same order. Neither, Smith says, are they to be conceived of as hoops to jump through. But an ideal Christian conversion will include them all.[15]

The first five elements of conversion are primarily internal. They include:

- **Belief.** A person needs to understand and agree with some basic facts about Jesus. For someone without a Christian upbringing, these may be things they previously didn't know. A person raised in a Christian family, on the other hand, might know and believe these things from infancy.

- **Repentance.** Conversion involves more than simple agreement with facts about Jesus. It means a change of mind and of direction. Repentance is not the same as sorrow or remorse. It is, in Gordon Smith's words, "a radical and unequivocal rejection of the way of sin and the pattern of life that leads to sin."[16]

- **Trust and assurance of forgiveness.** Responding to Jesus also touches our affections. A converted person will begin to grasp on an emotional level that God loves them and has forgiven them. This complements the more cerebral experience of "belief."

- **Commitment, allegiance and devotion.** As we encounter and get to know Jesus, we develop a determination to live for him in the world. Following him becomes more important than any other call on our lives. In fact, in the case of some of Jesus' first disciples, their conversion actually *began* with the missional call to become "fishers of men" (Mt 4:19 NASB).

- **The gift of the Spirit.** Our relationship with God ceases to be a relationship purely with an external reality. Instead, the Holy Spirit comes and takes up residence inside us. It is common for this to occur very early in the conversion process, but that is not always the case.

The other two aspects of Christian conversion are more outward. They are:

- **Baptism.** This is the "wedding ring" of the Christian. It doesn't place us in relationship with God, but it is the formal, outward symbol of the union that has taken place.[17]

- **Incorporation into the Christian community.** Most people first encounter Christ through the witness of another Christian or group of believers. It is essential that they eventually become fully participating members of the Christian community—insiders rather than outsiders.

This understanding of conversion is enormously helpful for engaging with some of the nominal Christians we have met in this chapter. Dave, the pioneer student leader, for example, had been incorporated into the Christian community and believed the essentials about Jesus. He had simply never turned to Jesus in repentance and trust, nor had he received the gift of the Spirit or assurance of forgiveness. Since these were his specific areas of need he was much more receptive when I called him to repentance and trust than he might have been to more detailed or traditional apologetic arguments.

The taxi driver, on the other hand, had only experienced one of the seven elements of conversion: baptism. His statement that "we cannot let our religion tell us how to live" indicated that he hadn't turned in repentance and devotion to Jesus. It also suggested that he didn't really apprehend the basic idea that God is in charge and we are not. Neither did he seem to think that submission to Jesus' leadership is even desirable. If he is to be fully converted, then, he needs more than the simple invitation I offered to Dave. He also needs to more accurately understand Jesus and the nature of relationship with him.

If conversion is this cluster of several experiences that occur in response to Jesus, then part of our role is to create ongoing opportunities for people to make these responses. All seven aspects of conversion

RETHINKING TESTIMONY

What kind of stories do you as an individual, or your church community, tell about conversion? Do you, and they, only spotlight the instantaneous aspects of coming to Jesus? Are there ways that you could adjust your storytelling to do justice to the fact that conversion is a process? Even if your stories focus on specific moments of response, perhaps you could describe these in the context of the longer-term spiritual journey. This would help give a more accurate understanding of following Jesus to those listening.

matter. Understanding them enables us to help walk others through their spiritual journeys and to focus our interactions on their specific areas of need.

Gordon Smith's framework also applies to our interactions with atheists and people who are spiritual but not religious. But it is especially relevant with nominals because they are more likely to have experienced at least *some* elements of Christian conversion, and therefore we will need to be especially attentive in focusing on their areas of need.

CONCLUSION

You meet nominal Christians every week. They are by the far the biggest group of the three featured in this book. Perhaps your temptation has been to see them as frauds, hypocrites or backsliders. For many people, though, the "Christian" aspect of their identity matters to them. They may even have experienced some aspects of Christian conversion. The Christian faith may be a source of pain as they recall the difficult relationships or unresolved doubts that pushed them from the church. Or, alternatively, Christianity could be something that has an impact on their lives even now and manifests itself in ways ranging from venerating saints to planting new Christian communities. The best way to find out what, if anything, Christianity means to them is to ask them to tell their story. Then perhaps you can be part of what happens next.

TAKING IT FURTHER

Do you know someone whom you consider a nominal Christian?
Into which of these categories do they fit?

- committed

- casual

- wanderer

- official

Which elements of conversion are missing from their experience?

- belief

- repentance

- trust and assurance

- commitment

- gift of the Spirit

- baptism

- church involvement

Take a moment now to pray for them to be fully converted. At
the end of your prayer ask God to bring to mind some ways he
might want to use you in this process, and make a note of these
responses:

QUESTIONS

Don't You Realize I've Been There and Done That?

h e was standing at the mouth of the dragon's cave. This was it. He'd spent many cold nights sleeping in unknown places, waded through wild rivers and scrambled over mountains so steep he'd lost his footing and feared it would all end right then. But it hadn't. He'd gone on to have many more unexpected adventures; he'd dodged forest fires, escaped traps and battled enemies, all to find the enchanted dagger that would forever rid the land of this winged menace.

The biggest surprise of all came right near the end of his long journey. He was close to giving up at that point. Hunger was consuming him. So he finally opened the package his grandfather had given him the day he left the village. Perhaps it had food in it. It might be stale, maybe even moldy, but he'd take anything at this point. As he wearily unwrapped the tight brown string from around the padded cloth, it began to unravel in his hand. Something fell, flashing in the moonlight as it did so. A chill worked its way rapidly along his whole body as he looked down and realized the truth: he'd had the dagger with him the whole time. He'd searched every corner of the land except for his own backpack. He reached down and, flooded with fear and excitement, wrapped his fingers around the dagger's handle.

TAKING A SECOND LOOK

It's a timeless story. A hero or heroine has been on a long quest to obtain something. In the end he or she discovers that the object of their search had been near in hand all along; in their house, pocket or even their own mind. The above story about the dagger isn't something I quoted; I actually wrote it myself. But you can find similar examples in all kinds of literature and film: Harry Potter's last horcrux, Dorothy's slippers in *The Wizard of Oz* and Dumbo's ability to fly without clutching his lucky feather are all famous examples. It resonates emotionally because we are all prone to disregard what is most familiar to us. One of the challenges of engaging with nominal Christians is that we are asking them to look afresh at things—Christianity, Jesus, church—with which they have been close, in name at least, but whose relevance and truth they have never fully grasped. We're asking them to open their own backpacks and take a second glance.

Some nominal Christians have never looked in the backpack of the Christian faith other than for a brief glimpse. They mistakenly assume familiarity with the basics of Christianity and function on this partial knowledge. Others have had more extensive contact with the church. They have a relatively accurate view of its teachings and practices and don't like what they have seen.

We'll need to help both groups take a fresh look at Jesus. Let's start by thinking about questions that tend to characterize those who've not looked at the basics of Christianity in depth or who have received it through the filter of faulty teaching. My friend Hannah is exactly this kind of person.

GOOD, HAPPY AND GODLESS

Hannah was, at most, a casual Christian. She wasn't hostile. As my friend she was pleased that I found it helpful to be a follower of Jesus.

But she didn't think it was for her. During our conversation I listened carefully to her opinions, and two particular lines jumped out at me. At one point she said, "I don't need God in order to be a good person." Later she added that "I can be happy without God."

She clearly felt she was able to be a joyful and ethical person without any help from God or religion. Hannah had grown up with occasional church attendance and also regular religious instruction at school. The values and morals taught by Jesus resonated with her, especially the Sermon on the Mount and parables such as the story of the good Samaritan.

As we talked I was very sympathetic to her viewpoint. She certainly was an upstanding person by most standards. She volunteered with the homeless and worked full time for a charity that helped asylum seekers. Her manner exuded joy and warmth. People felt drawn to her. I wish more Christians were like her in this respect.

My mind wandered to different ways I had heard Christians address situations like Hannah's. I remembered one particular preacher who said that we only *think* we are happy without Jesus because we don't realize the even deeper joy that is available in Christ. I'm not sure I completely disagree with him. But it wouldn't help me much here. Was I supposed to tell Hannah that she might think she's a joyful person but she's really not? She wouldn't buy it, and neither would I.

I also recalled a philosophy book I had read. It argued that the very concept of morality depends upon there being a God. It was a convincing argument. But, again, it sort of missed the point here. Hannah didn't reject Christianity on the grounds that we don't need God in order to have a concept of right or wrong. Instead she had noticed that she was ethically on par with most religious people and therefore decided that God didn't make that much difference.

Then something dawned on me. I realized that by focusing on morality or personal contentment we were both missing the point. Both Hannah and I were looking at Jesus through a faulty lens. And we weren't alone in this. Many people do the same thing.

The sociologist Christian Smith, whose National Study of Youth and Religion project has conducted in-depth interviews with thousands of young Americans, describes the outlook of most under-thirties on life as primarily "moralistic" and "therapeutic."[1] This means they perceive an ideal existence to be one in which they are focused on being a decent person and feeling good about themselves.

Many nominals like Hannah assume that Christianity is simply another "moralistic therapeutic" movement. That's why she assessed its value on the basis of whether it might improve her behavior or increase her happiness. When talking with someone like Hannah, we might be tempted to posit Christianity as morally superior or as the best source for future happiness. But doing so would be a mistake. There are, for sure, emotional and ethical dimensions to Christianity. But at its heart is a person and the call to respond to him.

My response to Hannah therefore ended up being quite a simple one. I asked her a question about Jesus. I felt as though moralistic and therapeutic issues were being treated as central, and Jesus was being pushed to the fringe. This needed to be reversed if she were to make any spiritual progress, so the question I asked her was whether she had read the teachings of Jesus.

She replied that it had been a while. But, she added, much of it had stuck in her mind. I noted that it seemed clear she had a pretty good grip on things Jesus had said about loving enemies, offering forgiveness and addressing poverty. But I suggested it still might be worth revisiting the Jesus narratives afresh as an adult. One thing that always strikes me about Jesus' teaching is that he isn't just giving instructions for behavior. So much of his teaching is actually about himself. I compared most religions' claim that "*this* is the way" with Jesus' statement "*I* am the way" (Jn 14:6). Jesus, unlike other moral and religious leaders, consistently crystallized the core issue of life as how we respond to him and not solely how we behave. I told Hannah that Jesus didn't describe our universe as simply a moral place. It is, even more importantly, a relational one. And a crucial aspect of existence, according to Jesus, is how we personally relate and respond to the one who made us.

We chatted a little more about this, and Hannah said she probably should take some time to revisit Jesus' teaching. I asked her if she might be up for reading Luke's Gospel over the next week, and then maybe we could grab lunch and she could tell me what she thought. Hannah thought this sounded great, so we got our phones out and arranged a time to meet.

EARNING YOUR WAY

Casual nominals like Hannah aren't the only ones who misunderstand Jesus as being focused primarily on behavior. Other more "committed" individuals also make a similar mistake. My friend Sami is just such an individual. We were talking over coffee once about Jesus, and he asked me, quite sincerely, "Does anybody else know about this 'grace' stuff, or is it just you and me?"

I was stunned into silence. He comes from a very strong church and a passionately Christian family. Could he really be unfamiliar with grace, the basic biblical doctrine that God welcomes us in spite of our failures and not because of our good works and obedience?

The minutes that followed revealed he'd not really understood how the entire burden of our salvation lies upon Jesus. His church, which was otherwise wonderful, put such an accent on the possibility of "falling away" that it had left him with the impression that he could only find favor with God through his own diligent efforts. So instead of turning trustingly toward Jesus, he was overwhelmingly focused on himself and his performance.

So, as I did with Hannah, I asked Sami a question about Jesus. This time I asked why he thought Jesus died. Simple, Sami replied immediately, he died because he loves us. I agreed. But why die to show this? Why not just send flowers? In my own words I repeated something I'd read in a John Stott book:

True love is purposive in its self-giving; it does not make random or reckless gestures. If you were to jump off the end of a pier and drown, or dash into a burning building and be burned to death, and your self-sacrifice had no saving purpose, you would convince me of your folly, not your love. But if I were drowning in the sea, or trapped in the burning building, and it was in attempting to rescue me that you lost your life, then I would indeed see love not folly in your actions. Just so the death of Jesus . . . must be seen to have had an objective, before it can have an appeal.[2]

"So," asked Sami, "what are you saying was Jesus' objective?"

I replied that maybe it was a rescue effort. Jesus himself said that he came "to seek and save that which was lost" (Lk 19:10 NASB). Jesus is called savior, rather than adviser, because his mission was to save and not simply suggest how we can redeem ourselves. He was diving into the nastiest "burning building" aspect of our reality—death—so that he might, through his resurrection, jump victoriously back out of the flaming window with us and all creation in his arms.

Sami was unconvinced and stuck to his viewpoint that we are saved through our own efforts. So I told him that if I thought salvation were through *my* own efforts I would be very worried. I know my own inconsistent track record well enough to not want anything as huge as my own salvation resting on it. I then asked him a personal question: "How about you? Do you feel confident that you are doing enough to secure your salvation? How's the works approach going for you?"

After looking down in a moment's contemplative silence, he admitted, "It's not going too well, actually." After another pause, he added, "So, maybe I should try your way instead."

"Yes," I laughed, "you probably should!"

These two foci—the saving death of Jesus and our own inability to match God's standards—often help those nominals who believe that the backpack contains the means to earn their own salvation.

NOT LIKING WHAT YOU HEAR

Sami and Hannah, then, had misperceived Christianity to be fundamentally about morality. Other nominals, however, are troubled not by such obvious misunderstandings but by core aspects of actual Christian teaching. In his research into "deconversion" from Christianity, Scot McKnight found that disagreement with specific Christian teachings plays a crucial part in many nominal Christians' drift away from the faith. Each individual wanderer has their own reservations about particular doctrines. But four specific areas of tension are more prevalent than any others:

• Scripture's reliability

• science and the Bible

• God of the Old Testament

• hell[3]

We need to be prepared to carefully consider and discuss each of these aspects of Christian teaching. It's worth remembering that Christians hold a range of views on each of the four questions. This doesn't mean that "nobody's right" or "it's all relative." But it does highlight that it is possible to be a follower of Jesus and to be still figuring these issues out. It doesn't have to be a barrier to faith if a person doesn't think every word of Scripture is inspired or that God created the universe on a particular timescale. One of the most helpful replies we can give to nominal Christians with concerns about specific Christian doctrines is, "Yes, that's a tricky issue; Christians debate that one too." We don't want to get sidetracked on internal theological discussions best left for later.

That said, however, if a person firmly feels one aspect of Christian teaching is not credible, then they are unlikely to consider the rest of it. They may never even get to engaging with Jesus. So we need to be able to intelligently address the above four aspects of Christianity, along with any others that may be on our friends' minds.

There are four dimensions to most difficulties nominals have with Christian doctrines:

Partial Understanding	Emotional Resistance	Intellectual Difficulties	Personal Consequences

Figure 11.1

Each of these dimensions can be seen clearly in the four major areas of doctrinal disagreement noted above. We can address an individual's concerns about Christian teachings more precisely if we listen carefully and identify which of the dimensions are on their minds. Each one requires a slightly different response.

Take, for example, the question of hell. Many objections to hell are based on a **partial understanding** of what the Bible and Christian theology teach about the topic. I have met many nominals who perceive that the church teaches people go to hell simply for not being Christians. Others believe that we are damned for failing to keep all the rules in God's big book.

An inaccurate perception of sin underpins many of these ideas. Sin is mistakenly viewed as holding the wrong religious affiliation or breaking specific commandments. The Bible, though, tends to paint sin in essentially relational terms. The prodigal son runs away with his father's money, Adam and Eve hide in the bushes, and Hosea's wife, Gomer, constantly cheats on him. Sin is about the personal rejection of God and his authoritative involvement in our lives.

Hell is a consequence of sin because God permits us to choose whether we will embrace or reject him. The biblical doctrine of hell teaches that if we choose to shut God out, he will one day honor our decision by shutting us out of his new creation. It's certainly a chilling outcome. But it's also one based on our decisions. As C. S. Lewis famously wrote, "The doors of Hell are locked on the inside."[4] It is our rejection of God and not his attitude to us that leads to the key being turned in hell's proverbial lock. Clarifying this point can help overcome many misunderstandings of hell.

As people consider hell they also experience **emotional resistance**. Their mental pictures of hell are frequently drawn from medieval paintings of pitchforked red demons roasting people over fires (or, at the very least, from relatively recent reinterpretations of these paintings in contemporary pop culture such as *The Simpsons* and Gary's Larson's *Far Side* cartoons).[5] They understandably find such images outrageous. Their incredulity only grows when they think of a deceased relative, perhaps a beloved grandmother or aunt, and recoil at the idea that this tender-hearted individual is currently turning on a spit over a smoldering sulfur pit.

We will need to do two things here. One is to dispel these cartoonish images of hell. The other is to move the focus away from their relatives and friends. We honestly have no idea where their relatives stood in relation to God. Whenever New Testament writers or Jesus mention hell they have a specific aim: to make readers and listeners consider the current trajectory of their own lives. We will similarly need to avoid entering into extended speculation about the eternal destinies of others' loved ones.

Hell also brings a range of **intellectual difficulties**. Not least among these is the question of whether hell is fair or proportionate. How can a loving God even contemplate such a thing? It seems so difficult an idea to reconcile with his kindness and grace.

What's needed here—once we've removed the caricatures of hell and shifted the focus away from where we think others might end up—is to rethink the nature of love. Does it, in fact, include respect for others and their decisions? Does it grant freedom to walk away, maybe even permanently?

If so, then hell is a mark of God's respectful permission that we can take him or leave him. We are permitted to say no and have that decision eventually rubber-stamped and finalized. There will obviously be consequences to declaring independence from the author of life. But the final decision rests in our hands.

Jerry Walls, a leading Christian philosopher who has written extensively about hell, describes "libertarian freedom" as "one of the main pillars of the orthodox Christian doctrine of hell."[6] He adds:

> [That] freedom is valuable may represent a ground-level intuition. As such it cannot easily be defended. . . . It is worth remarking, however, that placing an extremely high value on human freedom is not a Christian idiosyncracy. To the contrary, world-views as diverse as those of atheistic existentialism and process philosophy also place an extremely high value on human freedom. So it can at least be said that the Christian who appeals to the value of libertarian freedom to defend his belief in hell is making his case on the basis of a widely shared intuition.[7]

Doing away with hell, then, doesn't solve anything. It denies our liberty to say no to God. This is a freedom most people perceive themselves to possess and would be reluctant to relinquish.

A final reason why people shrink back from the idea of hell is the **personal consequences** of accepting the idea. The existence of hell implies that our choices in this life have ramifications beyond even death itself. Hell also reminds us that rejecting God is not a trivial matter. It pulls the rug from under our tendency to consider ourselves masters of our own destiny. We can point out to people that "if God is real and reaching out to us, then resisting that embrace is likely to have some consequences, don't you think?" Few will contest this sentiment. Then we can begin conversing a little more about how (and whether) God, through Christ, has stretched his arms toward us. It's a topic much more central to New Testament concerns than the question of hell.

This is just a brief demonstration of how the four dimensions of doctrinal difficulty relate to the concept of hell. You can use your own imagination to engage similarly with nominals' questions about other Christian teachings.

UGLY EXPERIENCES

It is not always ideas and doctrines that get in the way for nominal Christians. Sometimes their experiences of the church and its members have pushed them away. James, the doubting teenager who appeared in the previous chapter, drifted from church after developing a sense that it was not a place for people who ask awkward questions. This was primarily due to his church's internal culture. Barna Group president David Kinnaman says that James's experience is very common. His extensive research among former churchgoers reveals that their six most common criticisms regarding church culture are that it is:

- **overprotective**, with little space for "creativity and cultural engagement"

- **shallow**, offering only "easy platitudes, proof texting, and formulaic slogans"

- **antiscience**, failing to paint a constructive picture of how faith and science relate

- **repressive**, speaking about sexuality primarily in terms of rules about "dos and don'ts"

- **exclusive**, failing to be open-minded, tolerant and accepting

- **doubtless,** not carving out a safe space for people to express doubts and ask questions[8]

Other nominal Christians are not only concerned about things which happened *around* them in church. They are also carrying pain from what has happened *to* them. These range from simple mistreatment and unkindness right through the experiences of people like Renée Altson, who describes in her memoir how she was repeatedly raped by her fundamentalist father.[9] He said God told him to do it and would quote Scripture even as he abused her. It makes sense she'd run a mile from any church after that.

There's nothing we can do to reverse these past experiences. But we do have a chance to alter their future perspective of Jesus and his followers.

When we interact with nominal Christians we can become the face of the church to them. Their perspective on the church and on Jesus will begin to be recalibrated by what they see in us. Paul writes to the Corinthian church that "we are therefore Christ's ambassadors, as though God were making his appeal through us" (2 Cor 5:20). An ambassador's role is to be the physically present face and voice of the one who sent him or her.

This alone, however, tends not to remove the sense that the church—and, by extension, its message about Jesus—is undesirable. I have never seen anybody with a bad experience or impression of the church come to faith through interacting with a solitary Christian. It is, apart from anything else, all too easy for nominals to categorize the lone lovely Christian in their life as an anomaly, a one-off. It is only when they meet more Christians that they can begin to see a pattern and realize that perhaps their previous unhappy experiences are not representative of Christianity as a whole. This broadened contact with Christians can occur in informal settings as much as in church gatherings. When I first started in university campus ministry I saw a number of students come to faith through weekly house parties or even volleyball games. As they spent time with us and had fun, their previous negative view of Christians was adjusted.

These kinds of interactions will not have an impact, however, if we don't take time to assess whether we and our communities represent Jesus accurately. We need to ask hard questions of ourselves. Are the six accusations described by David Kinnaman true of *us*? Are we overprotective, shallow, antiscience, repressive, exclusive and doubtless? We each need to ask ourselves this question on an individual level. We also need to ask this of the communities that each of us helps lead. How could you adjust what you do in your family, your youth group, church, missional community, small group, Sunday school class or classroom to make them more culturally engaged, less simplistic, more constructive and holistic in relation to science and sexuality, and more welcoming of doubts and questions?

Fresh encounters with Christians, and also with communities of believers, can open nominals to rethinking their position on Jesus. But we will probably also need to speak in more detail about their personal experiences at some point. The temptation is to limit our response to saying, "Oh, but my church isn't like that." This is sometimes a helpful observation to make, especially when you are interacting with someone whose experience has been as extreme as Renée Altson's abuse by her father. But doing so does run the danger of painting a false contrast between your wonderful, perfect church community and the nominal Christian's negative experiences. The truth is that every church is broken in some way. Each one is a collection of sinners-made-saints. Flaws are inevitable. So on occasion I find it beneficial to apologize for the failings of the church as a whole before I say anything about my local church. You would be surprised how helpful it can be to say to someone with unpleasant church experiences, "I am so sorry that the church, of which I am a part, has done this." *Our* personal ownership of what happened to them often opens the door to *their* healing.

We can also be open about our own shortcomings. I have a friend who, when people say, "The church is full of hypocrites," always raises his hand in the air and says, "Yes, and I'm one of them." This may ring false if we are speaking to someone like Renée Altson. It will hardly build trust for us to compare our behavior with that of her abuser. But when speaking with those who have a generalized sense of the church's flawed nature that is not based on a single terrible experience, you can highlight that it's not just other people or communities that have shortcomings. We're all part of the same mess.

It can also be helpful to more directly raise the topic of Jesus. I often say, "For me, the interesting thing about Jesus is that he seemed to reserve his harshest words for some of the most religious folks. He called them things like a 'brood of vipers.' The bad stuff you have seen in church is as upsetting to him as it is to you." Other times, instead of explaining this aspect of Jesus, I simply ask, "What do you think Jesus would make of all this?" When nominal Christians start understanding that their church experience is not representative of all Christian communities, and when they spend time reflecting on the attitude of Jesus toward religious hypocrisy, it helps them reconsider their own attitude to him. A barrier is removed.

AVOIDING HYPOCRISY

A hypocrite is a person who projects an image of him- or herself that differs from reality. When Jesus calls people hypocrites it is usually because they are pretending to be a higher class of believer than those around them. They claim to be less sinful than is really the case (Mt 6:16; 23:27). They exempt themselves from the very call to holiness they are issuing toward others (Lk 6:42; 13:15). A true Christian shouldn't easily be a hypocrite because the entry point to knowing God includes admitting our sin and our need for a savior outside ourselves. Returning constantly to these basic biblical teachings on sin and grace (and permitting God to reshape us in light of them) will guard us from hypocrisy.

DENOMINATION HOPPING

One of the ironies of sharing Jesus with nominal Christians is that we can sometimes be perceived as pulling them away from the true faith. When conversing with people about Jesus, I have frequently sensed their fear that I may be attempting to make them switch Christian traditions. This is an especially acute concern for "casual" and "committed" nominal Christians. Their church affiliation often forms a significant dimension of their identity, and when they encounter someone who offers them a fresh take on Christianity they can easily assume that this person wants them to transfer from their current denomination.

If we sense that someone has this concern, we should try to be affirming of that person's particular denominational background. There are things to admire in all Christian groupings, whether they are Protestant, Roman Catholic or Orthodox. They all affirm the contents of the New Testament and also the Nicene Creed. Our priority is not that others change denominational identity but that they encounter and follow Jesus. When talking for the first time recently with somebody about Jesus, this person said—in an emphatic tone that was clearly designed to push me, the intruding evangelical, away—"I'm Eastern Orthodox." I simply replied, "I love the Orthodox, I'm reading a great book by an Orthodox theologian right now." Her hostility melted away before my eyes.

This question of church affiliation, though, is not as straightforward as this conversation suggests. Anybody who has visited enough churches will know that not all local Christian communities are marked by clarity on the essentials regarding Jesus and the message of the New Testament. Somebody in our denomination told me that she hadn't heard her pastor mention Jesus in a sermon for an entire year. Every week she thought it was going to happen. But in the end, she only heard mention of "God."

That's an extreme. But there are countless churches with a wildly inaccurate understanding of the gospel or an unhealthy internal culture. Nominalism is, in fact, frequently an outcome of churches getting it wrong. So, while we aren't primarily focused on church membership or denominational identity, we do need to be aware that a person's current church affiliation may not be the healthiest place for them to begin following Jesus. It could even be an impediment.

Finding a new local church may not, then, be the emphasis of our interactions. But, as the previous chapter noted, being part of a Christian community is a vital element of conversion. We want people to begin enjoying and experiencing church at some stage in their spiritual journey. This may entail introducing them to a new church community. If they are wanderers, casual or official Christians, in fact, it is very likely that their faith renewal will *require* this. For these groups, engaging with church, is not usually something that occurs after they begin following Jesus. The latter stages of most nominal Christians' journeys to faith actually take place *within* a local Christian fellowship, which we will explore further in the next chapter. For now it is sufficient to note that we will need to blend a verbally expressed warmth toward people's existing church affiliations with care to ensure that our own communities maintain a welcoming atmosphere.

INVITATION TO A QUEST

This chapter started with a hero on a quest. He had finally found the enchanted dagger and was now in a position to slay the dragon. If I were to expand this scene into a full-length novel, though, the blade's discovery would not form the final paragraph. It wouldn't even be in the last few chapters. Because the best bit of the story would be yet to come, the moment when he actually starts acting on what he had found. The hero's next move wouldn't be to drop the dagger and move on. Quite the opposite: he would grip it ever harder with each passing sentence.

As we help people rediscover Jesus, or even to take him seriously for the first time, they will hopefully also grow in their understanding of his significance. He will move from subplot to narrative focus. Perhaps in one of our conversations, our friends, like the tired journeyer seeing a flash of metal in the moonlight, will catch a glimpse of Jesus' importance. If this happens, then we will need to help them act on what they saw. The next chapter is all about helping them pick up the dagger and move on to the next stage of the adventure.

TAKING IT FURTHER

Think of a nominal Christian you know. Does the person:

- Assume he or she knows Christianity but really doesn't?

- Know Christianity and has therefore rejected it?

How do you think your answer to the last question should affect the way you pray and interact with this person?

What is his or her single biggest disagreement with basic Christian teaching?

- In what ways is the objection based on a misunderstanding of this teaching?

- Is the disagreement based on emotional resistance? How so?

- Do intellectual issues play a part in his or her holding this objection? Which ones?

- Do you think this person fears the personal consequences of agreeing with this teaching? What would those consequences be, and why might they fear them?

- If you had a ninety-second window in conversation to speak with him or her about this area of disagreement, what would you say? Write out your response in 150 words or less.

PRACTICES

Communities That Facilitate Rediscovering Jesus

THE GIFT

Diane left the room for a moment before returning and placing an old paperback in my mother's hands. "I think, Ann," Diane said with gentle conviction, "this may help you." My mother thanked her and slipped it into her bag.

After arriving home, my mother wasn't completely surprised to discover that the book was about God. Her friendship with Diane had begun, after all, at the local Quaker Meeting House. My mother had recently begun attending Sunday worship regularly for the first time in over a decade. As a result of miscarriage and clinical depression, she had reached a point of wanting to reassess her life. Church seemed like the natural place to do so.

Mum had grown up religious. Her father, Eric Robertson, was a missionary to India renowned both for bridging cultural divides and being "delighted to witness" about "the gospel of Jesus Christ."[1] She was just six years old when he died, and she flew back to England with her mourning mother and three siblings.

Within a few years she was sent to a Quaker boarding school with daily acts of worship. She says that this warmly religious educational environment, combined with memories of her late father's passionate faith, meant that she never considered herself anything other than a Christian.

So it was natural for her to visit the local Quaker congregation in times of trouble. Diane, like my mother, was also a newcomer. They swiftly connected and arranged for their children to play together. Diane spoke little about God, but she did listen well. My mother says there was an attractive strength and calm about her new friend. Until this friendship, my mother later explained to me, "God had just been an abstract idea or someone whose existence I affirmed." She hadn't given him much thought since leaving her boarding school.

The little Christian paperback Diane had given her turned out to be a revelation. It spoke of knowing God personally in a relationship. There was an explanation of how to bring our sins to Jesus, and that he would forgive them. My mother was so amazed by this possibility that she put down the book, grabbed a pen and paper, wrote a list of her sins, and then found a quiet place and read her list to Jesus.

This simple act was a turning point for her. After almost thirty years of respecting Christianity from an arm's distance, she now found herself regularly talking to Jesus about the things happening in her life. If he could handle her sins, she figured, then he could probably cope with everything else going on in her life.

In the years that followed, she experienced healing from depression and was unexpectedly able to have two more children. She became an active church member, and all her offspring themselves became followers of Jesus. My father also had his own conversion experience. But it all began with Diane's gift.

My mother's story is unique. So is everybody else's. But it contains three elements that are present in almost every nominal Christian's journey to faith:

- rediscovering Jesus (in the book)
- encountering community (through Diane at the Quaker meeting)
- making a response (through taking a list of sins to Jesus)

In this chapter you'll discover ways you can help the nominal Christians in your life experience each of these elements.

Mini-Practice: Reading a Gospel with a Friend

My close friend and former ministry colleague Krisztina Mair recently described for me a memorable scene that unfolded in her kitchen. She was sitting on a stool, a half-eaten piece of cake on the plate in front of her. To her left was some printed text from the New Testament, and her steaming coffee mug on the right was still almost full. But Krisztina's mind was on neither food nor drink nor Bible. She was instead looking in amazement at her longtime friend Chloe, who'd just asked something utterly unexpected: "Can we pray?"

Krisztina was as surprised to hear the question as Chloe was to ask it. Just five weeks previously Chloe would never even have thought about the topic of prayer. But she had become increasingly curious about Krisztina's attitude to life. Krisztina had experienced the divorce of her parents and later the death of her beloved stepfather. Recently she had been in a brutal car crash, and her back required ongoing therapy. But somehow Krisztina still exuded joy. Chloe was intrigued.

Things had begun to snowball when Chloe finally asked Krisztina about the source of her contentment. Krisztina's reply, that it was "because of Jesus," had sparked some lively conversation. Chloe had some fleeting past church connections and considered herself a Christian rather than anything else. But she had never really looked in detail at Jesus. Krisztina suggested that it might be helpful for them to read some of the stories of Jesus together and discuss them. Chloe agreed.

So began a series of weekly chats over cake where the focus of conversation was a passage from Luke's Gospel. Each Tuesday evening they sat in Krisztina's kitchen, ate cake, drank coffee and talked Jesus. Over the course of their time together the source of Krisztina's joy had become increasingly tangible, desirable and plausible to Chloe. Now she wanted to know and follow Jesus for herself. That's when she asked the unanticipated question "Can we pray?"

Krisztina was taken aback because she hadn't realized that Chloe, for so long indifferent to all things Christian, had changed her outlook so profoundly in such a short time. But despite her surprise, Krisztina had experienced such scenarios before. She'd previously sat down to read the New Testament Jesus narratives with many people and had seen a range of responses. Some conversation partners had begun to follow Jesus afterward. Others simply had their curiosity fueled and remained to be convinced. But the conversations had always resulted in some kind of impact.

I recently asked Krisztina what led her to this practice of reading the Jesus stories with others. She told me the habit began when she was hired as a student pastor at her local church immediately after graduating from college. As she got to know the young people who attended each week, she swiftly began to realize that she had no idea where most of them stood in relation to Jesus.

So she began inviting some of them to sit down with her for an hour each week to have a casual conversation about a segment from one of the Gospels. Students soon began coming to faith. Others had their relationships with God assume new levels of vibrancy. Yet, for all this impact, Krisztina tells me that it didn't feel like hard work. "I didn't need to convince many of them," she told me, "because the text seemed to do that work for me."

This, according to Krisztina, is part of the beauty of reading the Bible with others: "Jesus just walks off the pages and people meet him for themselves; then they can either embrace him or reject him." It's such an informal practice, really just a conversation between two friends with a prearranged topic on the table. It resembles Agnostics Anonymous with a Bible focus and reduced to two or three participants.

Even people who would not consider attending church often feel remarkably at ease sitting and wagging chins over a story about Jesus.

Part of Krisztina's current ministry role is to equip others in this practice of reading through a Gospel with a friend. When Krisztina and I last spoke, she came up with a list of eight helpful tips that might help anyone who wants to start reading the New Testament Jesus narratives with another person.

Be unafraid. Don't hedge your invitation. Tell them what you have in mind, and that you think it would be good for them to check out the evidence for themselves. When you meet, remain unafraid; it doesn't matter whether you know all the answers, just admit when you don't. The idea here is not for you to download all your expertise on the topic of Jesus. Instead, you are opening the pages of his story and letting others encounter him. He will be the one who does the work for you.

Agree on the schedule. Ideally, meet between four and six times together, forty-five to sixty minutes each time. This will give people the opportunity to explore Jesus in sufficient depth. Krisztina usually proposes an initial meeting to discuss one passage, and then if they enjoy that conversation, she suggests, "If you really want to make sense of Jesus, then there are six stories about him which will help you gain a clearer picture. Why don't we meet again and look at the next passage?"

Pick passages carefully. It helps to know ahead of time which passages you will look at over your weeks together. Krisztina tends to follow, in order, the series of passages selected by Rebecca Manley Pippert for her excellent *Uncovering the Life of Jesus* seeker discussion guide.[2] Together these six passages provide a great introduction to the story of Jesus:

- introduction to Luke's Gospel and the healing of the paralyzed man (Lk 1:1-4; 5:17-26)
- Jesus and the sinful woman (Lk 7:36-50)
- parables of the lost sheep and lost son (Luke 15:1-3, 11-32)

- the blind man and Zacchaeus (Lk 18:35–19:10)
- Jesus' death and trial (Lk 22:66-71; 23:13-25, 32-56)
- Jesus' resurrection (Lk 24:36-49)

Read the text beforehand. Spend some time prior to each meeting looking through the given Gospel text you will discuss. Try to discern aspects of it that will likely trigger questions for your friend or that will be difficult for you to explain. Consider how you might be able to help your conversation partners make sense of potentially tricky bits.

Be yourself. You may be tempted to go into "Bible study mode" or begin speaking or acting unnaturally. Instead, relax. You don't need to open or close in prayer. Treat the gathering instead as just another conversation, albeit one that has an agreed focal point. Meet in a natural and relaxed place—a home, bar or coffee shop, for example— where you would normally meet for an in-depth chat with a friend. If you're at ease, they will be too.

Prepare questions. You don't have to start cold and sit wondering what to say. You can have some questions ready. Krisztina says she and her conversation partner normally begin by each reading slowly and silently though the passage. Then Krisztina asks simple text-focused, conversation-opening questions such as:

- "What stands out to you?"
- "What surprises you?"
- "What is difficult to make sense of?"

They then each share their thoughts and answers on these topics; it should flow like any other conversation. An alternative approach is to ask the other person to read the passage ahead of time. Give them a printout of it on a sheet of paper so they can scribble and annotate their thoughts. Tell them, "Let's both read this, make a list of questions and thoughts, and then we'll discuss those together when we next meet."

End with invitation. When you have your final session together, have a chat about their next steps. Ask them whether they are ready to make a decision to follow Jesus. If they are, then walk them through the step of praying and welcoming him into their lives. Be sure to meet again soon after to follow up on that decision and begin helping them continue their new life with Christ.

Be openhanded. Don't apply any pressure if they don't want to make that decision. Simply ask whether they are hesitating because of something they don't believe or something they don't understand.[3] Make clear that it is fine to stop meeting, but also offer the possibility of continuing to meet and focus the topics and choices of future passages around their particular concerns. Let *them* decide what happens next.

Both Krisztina and I agreed that reading a Gospel together is the best next step for nominals who are interested and want to find out more. In Krisztina's words, it creates "a context in which misperceptions about Jesus can be stripped down and the real Jesus is permitted to creep into the imagination." It happened with Chloe in a kitchen smelling of freshly baked cake. Maybe something similarly extraordinary could also occur in one of the everyday settings of your life.

MESO PRACTICE: STORY LISTENING

Reencountering the story of Jesus, then, is an essential facet of most nominal Christians' journey to full conversion. But his isn't the only story that matters. We also need to create space for nominals to share and reassess their own life narratives so they can explore how Jesus might fit into them.

I was struck by the power of listening to nominals' stories recently when I saw a casual Christian shift from being very skeptical to sincerely seeking in the course of just twenty-four hours. We were at a ski camp for college students organized by a campus ministry. About half those attending were nominal Christians. Each morning, between breakfast and hitting the snowy slopes, students heard a short TED-style talk designed to provoke thought and discussion throughout the day. In the evenings we met in smaller groups to discuss the talk and also look at a New Testament passage from the life of Jesus.

In my first evening discussion group, Ciprian—a nominally Eastern Orthodox student—spent our whole time together throwing out a series of objections to the Christian faith. Science, psychology, Old Testament genocides and almost every other question covered in this book came out of the bag. He positioned himself to us as an extreme skeptic. We listened patiently and tried our best to offer helpful answers. But every time a Christian moved beyond affirming his question to addressing it, Ciprian switched topics and raised another objection. Something suggested he wasn't too interested in our answers. We wondered whether he was just playing with us.

The next night in our discussion group, Ciprian began as expected. He launched into a series of fluent eye-rolling statements against Christianity. At one moment, when he paused for breath, I jumped in and asked, "Ciprian, these are great questions you're raising, but I don't feel like they're *your* questions. I'd love to know what *you* think about God."

Ciprian's whole demeanor changed and after a lengthy pause he replied, "What I think? Honestly, I am confused. To be considered smart, I feel I need to be a skeptic or an atheist, but I've had these experiences which I've never told anyone about." And for the next half an hour we heard about his tales of prayer and spiritual oppression in the family. He opened up honestly about his sense of desiring God and also fearing him. We all listened and asked many questions. At the end of our conversation Ciprian said warmly, "I've never told anyone any of that stuff, but you guys took my questions last night so seriously that I began to think maybe I could trust you with this."

The shift was subtle. It was no instant conversion. But it did mark the moment when he transitioned from holding all Christians at arm's length to considering us the kind of people with whom he could explore his own spiritual journey. Note that Ciprian's change of attitude didn't occur primarily because he listened to the stories of others or heard their thoughtful answers to his questions. It was instead catalyzed by being given space to share his own stories and air his perspective on the Christian faith.

This space for sharing personal stories is vital for engaging nominal Christians. My friend Rick Richardson, author of the insightful books *Reimagining Evangelism* and *Evangelism Outside the Box*, says that nominals often ask the same questions as atheists. But he says they do so for different reasons. Atheists tend to be curious whether Christians have robust answers to their questions. Nominals, on the other hand, often pose questions as a way of testing whether Christians and churches can handle their doubts and disagreements. Their concern is more about whether they fit in rather than whether we have the answers. Ciprian felt safe and connected with us because we welcomed his questioning and took his perspective seriously. We may still need to address his questions at some point, but they were not the most important issue.

Stefan Paas, a church planter in the Netherlands, says that many contemporary Western nominals such as Ciprian treat the church quite differently from those who grew up regularly involved in a local church. He writes:

People with a [churched] background have been raised with the idea of church as a family. Families stick together. People show up at parties and celebrations, even if they don't like them. That's what family members do for one another. They are connected by loyalty, duty, and (hopefully) love. Most other people . . . view church as a restaurant. It is a place you go when you are in the mood—in other words, when you feel a spiritual need. You may like this particular restaurant very much, but that does not imply that you will return next week . . . sometimes a quick snack is just as good, and often it is easier and cheaper to eat at home.[4]

Most nominals, Paas is saying, come to church with no intention of regular, ongoing involvement with either the congregation or Jesus. Paas suggests we should respond to this shift with kindness and understanding, by becoming "relaxed with irregular guests," and by avoiding creating undue pressure for further commitments.[5] We'll also, though, need to create moments when visitors can transition from occasional "customers" to "family members" who consider our community the home base for their ongoing spiritual explorations. Making room for them to tell their own stories and share their experiences is an ideal way to do this. It can, as Rick Richardson says, help them probe whether we are a community within which their ongoing life narrative fits. This is vital because, as the last chapter noted, it is from *within* a Christian community that most nominals begin following Jesus.

Space for stories is best created either in personal conversations or in the mid-sized gatherings of the church, such as Alpha, Christianity Explored, small groups, women's or men's events and youth groups. These are the settings in which it is easiest to have an open discussion where everyone can join in, but where people also feel free to sit and quietly listen.

If you want to create space for story listening in your context, then you'll need the following five items:

- **Genuine interest.** It just won't work to ask about a person's story or experience as a pretext for slipping in your pre-prepared message. They'll sense the inauthenticity of the moment. Instead, cultivate a genuine care for them and their stories. It's important that you *want* to hear what they have to say.

- **Early timing.** Don't *wait* to hear others' stories. At the first opportunity make space for people to share a little about where they are coming from and what they think. The longer you wait the more you risk them jumping to the (hopefully false) conclusion that your Christian community isn't a place for people like them.

- **Crafted prompts.** Think carefully about how you can invite their stories. Weave it around the topics you are discussing together. When I speak to college students on passages in which Jesus confronts religious leaders, for example, I will almost always begin by inviting those present to share their worst experiences of religion.

This both shows interest in their stories and also lets them open up the part of their lives to which my subsequent talk is most relevant.

- **Active listening.** Resist the temptation to leap in with your thoughts and responses. But don't stay silent either. Use eye contact, nod and occasionally ask questions. Help draw out more clearly what they want to say.

- **Integrative interpretation.** When they have finished speaking, summarize and affirm what they have said, then verbally connect it to the wider context of your church or Christian community. Briefly note how it fits in with what you are doing together. In Ciprian's case, for example, I said, "So, Ciprian has had all these experiences and isn't sure what he believes now. I think it's great he's been so honest, because this camp and this community is intended to be a group of people figuring out together what they make of Jesus."

Story listening can be a great tool for helping nominals make the step from restaurant customer to family member. It brings their stories into a context where the narrative of Jesus is also being discussed. And good things can happen when the two stories, theirs and Jesus', brush up against each other for the first time.

MACRO PRACTICE: INVITING A RESPONSE

Rediscovering Jesus and seeing a community listen well to newcomers are both vital practices for engaging nominal Christians. As these things happen, though, we want to do more than simply convey information or welcome people into our midst. We also need to invite them to personally turn to him in repentance and faith, a step that is often overlooked. We assume that people will somehow slip into following Jesus. Understanding conversion as a process, which was an emphasis of chapter ten, sometimes leads Christians to underplay the importance of specific moments of invitation for response.

We are rightly wary of falling into the trap of shrinking the whole spiritual journey down to one brief moment of decision. But even long physical journeys involve important passing moments. There are key choices when we turn left or right, times when we consult the map and determine our route. These may last mere minutes, but they set our direction for far longer. Spiritual journeys follow the same pattern. They are ongoing processes that include significant moments of reorientation. And part of our role is to invite people into those moments.

One of my friends, York Moore, told me a story about how he discovered the importance of invitation during his student days. He was a brand-new Christian, a philosophy undergraduate from an atheist background who was saved during an attempted suicide. His miraculous encounter with Jesus catapulted him into a life of passionately sharing his faith with others.

One day he found himself in the library with a classmate, Chris, and conversation turned toward the question of Jesus. York says that he had an amazing opportunity to explain the message of Jesus and his own life story in great depth. He describes it as the most complete articulation of the gospel he had ever achieved. Chris was clearly affected by what they had discussed. But they reached a point when York had no idea what else to say. Silence fell. An awkward and unresolved tension hung in the air. Then Chris opened his mouth and asked a question that terrified York. He asked, "Okay then, what next?"

York says he was completely unprepared for this question. Up until this point he had conceived of evangelism as conveying information to which people would hopefully respond. Now he realized that part of his responsibility, when introducing friends to Jesus, was to outline for them clearly *how* they could actually turn and entrust their lives to him. Information mattered. But it was also important to help people act on that information.

In the years that followed, York made invitation a key feature of his personal conversations with others. He would encourage friends to actually take the step of trusting Jesus for themselves. Several decided to do so. As he began to be increasingly prominent as a public speaker, especially on college campuses as a national evangelist for InterVarsity, York made sure that his presentations always addressed the key question he first heard in that college library: "Okay then, what next?" Over the past two decades he has seen literally thousands of people come to faith in Christ in response to his invitations.

When York told me his story, I asked him about the place of invitation for response in a local Christian community such a church or campus group. I could see how it is important for a traveling evangelist who only meets his audience a few times. They only have a few opportunities to extend that invitation. But how would it work in an ongoing community setting like a church or a campus group? I was especially concerned about how it might push away wanderers who left the church precisely because they felt it always pressing for people to "pray the prayer."

York agreed with me that an ongoing local community setting was slightly different from an enormous one-off event. He, as the chair of elders at his local church, is currently working through exactly this issue. One of his current conclusions is that inviting response is as important in a local congregation as it is anywhere else. People still need to turn to Christ and trust him. We must not avoid the "Okay, what next?" question. Instead we should be creative in how we address it.

I asked York for the most important pieces of advice he would give to someone looking to creatively extend an invitation for response to nominal Christians and others in a larger group setting such as a Sunday service, Alpha course or weekend retreat. York gave me five key pointers:

- First, you must be very careful to phrase your invitation in a way that makes clear that you are inviting people to make a response to Jesus. It is a huge danger that people will mistakenly hear our call to response as an ultimatum regarding whether or not they can still be part of our community. We need to be clear to people that we value having them be part of our life and that we want them to continue to feel at home with us. We love them being with us, and that welcome is set to continue whatever they decide. But we are simply creating an opportunity to respond to Jesus if this is their moment to do so.

- Second, explicitly link your invitation to things they may have already experienced up until this point. It is vital that your invitation feels like a natural continuation of their life journey until now. Think carefully about the people present. Have they mostly been involved in your community for just a few weeks or months? Then say something such as, "You've been getting to know some of us here, seeing what following Jesus looks like in real life, and perhaps you are thinking of beginning that process for yourself. We just want to carve out a little space here you can take that step."

- Third, with nominal Christians we will want to avoid the language of "becoming a Christian," as this is confusing to people who already use that term to describe themselves. York instead draws the contrast between "acquaintance" and "embrace," saying, "You have gotten to know about God, but now might be a good time to actually say 'yes' to him and welcome him into your life."

- Fourth, design a mode of response that is concrete and memorable. Be clear and precise about the kind of response you are inviting. Do more than suggest they pray a prayer and then go home. When York spoke at the Urbana Student Missions Convention a few years ago, his message was about being the light of the world. He invited people to follow Jesus and begin shining for him in the darkest parts of the world. Ushers around the conference hall had glowsticks, and at the end of his message, with the lights dimmed, York invited those present to mark their response to Jesus by taking a stick, cracking it and causing it to shine in the darkness. As the room filled with pinpricks of radiant color, many people saw the moment illustrated by indelible visuals.

- Fifth, make a focus of your appeal what life looks like afterwards. The next phase of life may be a continuation of what has gone

before, York said, but it will also include some changes. York sometimes says, "God, who has until now been at the fringes of your life
will now move to center; he'll begin influencing you from the
inside." The temptation is to just get people to "sign up" and agree
to more clearly self-identify as Christian. The more clearly we can
describe life with Christ, the better.[6]

Following Jesus requires a response on our part. York's advice is a real
help in thinking through how we can invite others to make that response for themselves without giving the impression that not doing
so will end their welcome in our community.

Few nominal Christians are insincere about their religious identity.
It means something to them. But they still need to encounter Jesus
and respond to him. Krisztina and York have offered some great
pointers for making this happen. But as Rick highlights, the bridge
between understanding Jesus and responding to him is frequently a
community where they feel at home. It is from within such intimate
settings that many nominal Christians become open to encountering
Jesus for themselves.

TAKING IT FURTHER

Think again of one nominal Christian you know. Are they currently experiencing any of these:

- Christian community

- investigating Jesus

- invitation to response

Which of the three should they experience next/first? Pause to
pray and think about this your answer to this.

How might that happen, and what might your role be? Pause
again to pray and think about your answer to this.

Adventures with Ukrainian Comic Book Jesus

N o! Don't stop reading yet. I know that final chapters are often needless space fillers. But this one will be worth your time. I promise. Do you remember Nasrin? She was the Swedish bisexual atheist mentioned briefly in chapter nine. It turns out there was more to her story than just a few conversations about difficult questions. Her tale is quite amazing. It begins with a simple question: "Should I do it today?"

NASRIN'S STORY

Nasrin was sat on the edge of her bed pondering whether this was the moment to kill herself. Every morning she awoke and contemplated ending her life.

Just one thing held her back. Pinned to her bookshelf was a crumpled paper picture no bigger than a cigarette pack. An unexpected gift from another member of the commune where she lived. Seeing it always made her hit pause on ending it all and convinced her to give the day a chance.

She was just twenty-three years old. But her biography was a long one. It had started out by being born to a Persian family in Tehran, Iran. Over the next six years her parents moved her to Turkey, Spain and eventually Sweden. By the time she reached this final stop her father had become an Islamic fundamentalist. He began preparing her for life as a dutiful Muslim wife.

She imbibed Islam and believed it wholeheartedly until she was taken into foster care at the age of thirteen after problems at home. Then a shift began. As her teens kicked in, she found that she was living in a tension between the demands of God and her own incapacity to fulfill them. She came to the conclusion that God was a tyrant. He commanded an obedience of which she was incapable. So she lost patience. At sixteen years old she told God that she didn't want to believe in him anymore. She felt relieved, and she was happy to be rid of him.

As the years continued, she shifted into an ever-angrier form of opposition to religion. Her boyfriend, an aficionado of New Atheist author Sam Harris, further fueled her fury toward God. Their relationship also hardened her intellectual confidence in atheism. She had come to realize that without the transcendent there could be no meaning in life, not objectively.

Her college philosophy lecturers told her that we have to make our own meaning. But this seemed to her like a mere game. Just because you decide something gives your life value doesn't mean that it does. The only honest response to atheism, she felt, was hopelessness and depression. Anything else was denial. It was a short bridge from here to sitting on the edge of the bed wondering whether to end it all. Why carry on if it's all meaningless?

But then there was that crumpled picture. She'd assumed it was a joke when she first unfolded it. Her roommate, a fellow atheist with Buddhist leanings, had bought it on a trip to the Ukraine. He said he'd had a strange compulsion to purchase it for her.

She'd taken it from his hand, opened it up and saw what seemed to her like a comic book drawing of Jesus. Clearly her friend was poking gentle fun at her hostility to religion. She pinned it up among the eclectic mix of other pictures on her bookshelf.

Then something strange began to happen. She told me later that "every time I looked at it, I felt a bit lighter; all this darkness became lighter, better . . . I couldn't explain it and I thought it was crazy, but I couldn't afford to deny anything, so I kept it up on the shelf."

This experience kept repeating with every glance its way. So she went to the library and borrowed a book on Jesus. The author, a Lutheran archbishop, described a God who "went out to court people and win people over." It was quite unlike the images of God with which she had been raised. It was genuinely desirable. Yet she was still convinced about her atheism. Jesus may have affected her through the painting, which was actually a famous work called *The Sacred Heart of Jesus*, and through the archbishop's book. But, from an intellectual standpoint, nothing religious could ever be a serious option for her.

One night, after another day of choosing life over death, Nasrin was alone in her room. She says that she "suddenly felt that there was someone in the room with me, like when a person walks behind your back and you sense their presence even though you haven't seen or touched them."

She instantaneously found herself drenched with the most intense feelings of her life. It was, she says, "like when you fall in love, but all those feelings came at once and surrounded me and filled me." A series of words began sweeping through her mind with intense clarity. There was an almost poetic rhythm as she heard:

I exist,
I love you,
live through me,
rest in me,
there is meaning,
don't give up.

This cycle of phrases repeated over and over in the same order "until I got the message." Then, as abruptly as it arrived, the presence left and the words stopped.

She was stunned and soon reached for some kind of rational explanation. Was she losing her mind? She hadn't realized that God did home visits. Especially not to the suburbs of Stockholm. But hang on ... this couldn't be God. At least not the one with whom she was raised. He would never be so personal as to say those things.

Then she remembered the one other place she had experienced even an echo of such tangible joy and peace: the Ukrainian picture of Jesus. So Jesus now became the focus of her investigations about God. Over the next year she borrowed even more books about him from the library. She held back from suicide because of the tantalizing possibility that her experience represented something real. This glimmer of hope restrained her. But, in her words, "just because it feels good doesn't mean it's true." Plausibility was still lacking.

Finally she came across a book written by Stefan Gustavsson. So she googled him, discovered his apologetics academy and dropped him an email, and their friendship began. She still considered herself an atheist and hadn't relinquished her hostility to God. But she was now ready to talk with someone who might be able to answer her questions. Twelve months later she was a follower of Jesus.

EVANGELISM *WITH* GOD

Nasrin's story is striking. I feel chills just writing it. But it's more than just an arresting tale. It also contains a feature common to almost every spiritual journey: something unexpected occurs that no human being planned. Nasrin was inexplicably drawn by a piece of art purchased for her on a similarly mysterious impulse. Soon thereafter her bedroom was flooded with the presence of God, and his love for her was communicated directly.

We could pick out similar features from many of the stories in this book. Tamara, in chapter two, began to take God seriously after listening to a piece of classical music. Martin Smith found that a church altar call resonated with a song lyric lodged in his brain. Dave, the pioneering student leader from chapter ten, only noticed God's absence when he lapsed in his church attendance.

None of these are things you could engineer. Would you ever think to give an atheistic, bisexual, ex-Muslim a slightly cheesy piece of religious art? Suggest that an apparently committed Christian quit church? Tell a lapsed Catholic that she should probably just put on a classical CD? These are counterintuitive moments that even the most insightful evangelist would be unlikely to foresee. Without them, however, there is no turning point in any of these stories.

As we come to the end of a book suggesting ways to adjust your practice, it's helpful to remember that what you and I do is not the whole story. Far from it. One of my mantras in life is something Nicole Voelkel (from chapter six) told me back in that Wisconsin pub. She said that "evangelism is something we do *with* God and not just *for* him." He is doing the work and we, in the words of Rick Richardson, are just his "junior partners."[1]

Repeat that to yourself a few times: "*with* God and not *for* God." Tattoo it on your mind. Yet don't overlook the fact that evangelism—communicating about Jesus in a way that invites others to follow him—is still something *we* need to do, even if it's not a task we undertake alone.

Note that Nasrin didn't renounce her atheism until almost two years after the incredible experience in her bedroom. That moment shattered her indifference to God and opened her mind to new possibilities. But she still couldn't honestly, as a thinking person, bring herself to affirm the existence of God. She still needed her questions answered, and this only happened after meeting Stefan. Nasrin went so far as to tell me that if it weren't for those detailed conversations she wouldn't have ever taken the step to follow Jesus for herself. Stefan was indispensable. He just wasn't the whole story.

This is exactly what the New Testament leads us to expect. Paul says that he "planted the seed, Apollos watered it, but God has been making it grow" (1 Cor 3:6). Plants sprout and flower through their own biological processes. It's not your responsibility to convert people any more than it is your job to stand all day with your hand in a flowerpot trying to make tulip bulbs blossom. Yet, even if you don't physically make plants grow, you can still encourage or inhibit their development. Watering and planting matter. You have some influence. The greater part of the work is with God. But not one ounce of energy you put into making Jesus known is ever wasted.

Good will always result when we're doing evangelism *with* God. He's the author of the unanticipated. He unsettles our expectations by speaking through Ukrainian paintings of Jesus and making house visits to the suburbs of Stockholm. Take confidence in the fact that as you sow, and your friends water, God will also be working to make things grow in whatever context you find yourself.

TAKING IT FURTHER

In this book you have encountered a range of practices. What one practice struck you as most immediately doable?

Take a few minutes to sketch out the series of steps you need to take in order to implement it.

What one apologetic question in this book did you wish you could understand and answer better?

What resources will you use to help you with this question?

Comparative Statistics for Canada and the United Kingdom

CANADA

Canadians identify as Christians almost as much as US residents, but they are significantly less likely to attend church (see pp. 24-25 for US statistics):[1]

67% of the Canadian population
described themselves as "Christian" in 2011

21% of the Canadian population
attended church on a weekly basis in 2005

This suggests that a large chunk of the Canadian population consists of nominal or inactive Christians.

Spirituality without religious affiliation is also common:[2]

50% of Canadians considered
themselves religious in 2012

65% of Canadians considered
themselves spiritual in 2012

Belief in God is also lower than in the United States. Canadians are more likely to be atheist than US residents:[3]

11% of the Canadian population
were atheist in 2009-2010

UNITED KINGDOM

Brits come even lower in terms of church attendance and self-identification as Christian. Here are the most optimistic figures available:[4]

59% of the United Kingdom
population described themselves
as "Christian" in 2011

10% of the United Kingdom
population attended church
on a weekly basis in 2007

Considering oneself a Christian, then, does not necessarily lead to church involvement in the United Kingdom. Nominal Christians are common. Despite such low attendance figures, however, there is still spiritual interest beyond the churches:[5]

42% of the United Kingdom
population said in 2007 that
they sometimes pray

19% of United Kingdom
population described themselves as
spiritual but not religious in 2013

A substantial minority of Brits are effectively atheistic:[6]

33% of the United Kingdom
population didn't believe in
God or a higher power in 2015

Did God Command Genocide?

If Oana (in chapter five) had wanted to talk detail about Old Testament atrocities, then I would have suggested we talk through whatever specific passage(s) she had in mind. A few days after meeting Oana, for example, I spent an hour talking over coffee with another student who was troubled by the portrait of the plague-sending God in Exodus. There was no way to unravel his questions except through detailed discussion of the text he had read. You'll also need to be willing to dive into a text if necessary; perhaps if you don't know much about the passage under discussion, you can just listen to their questions and criticisms and promise to do some thinking and research on them before coming back and offering a thoughtful response.

If Oana had no particular passage in mind, or if there were several that bothered her, then I would likely have suggested we speak about the very controversial passage from Deuteronomy where it says of seven nations, including the Amorites, that Israel "must destroy them totally. Make no treaty with them, and show them no mercy" (Deut 7:2). It appears to be a command to commit genocide and tends to be the focus of many arguments against the goodness of the Bible.

I would probably have shared with Oana some of the following thoughts:

- Amorites were not a good, innocent people. They worshiped the god Molek by sacrificing their children to him in the fire (Lev 18:21; 20:2-4; 2 Kings 23:10; Jer 32:25).

- This aspect of Amorite religion was catching on among surrounding nations. It was threatening to become a feature of the culture as a whole (Lev 18:21; 1 Kings 11:5, 33). It was a danger to everyone, and not just the Amorites.

- God first mentions his war plans against the Amorites a full four hundred years before implementing them (Gen 15:16). It is not, then, a grumpy, impulsive move. It is a slow one that affords the Amorites plenty of time to change their ways.

- The phrase "destroy them totally" doesn't necessarily imply genocide. It was common in the ancient Middle East for warfare to be described in very extreme terms. Instead of stating calmly and measuredly "We will win this war," they would shout "We'll annihilate every one of them." In 1230 BC, Pharaoh Merneptah said, "Israel is wasted, his seed is not."[1] Mesha, king of Moab, boasted in 830 BC that "Israel has utterly perished for always."[2] Both phrases suggest complete annihilation to modern ears. Yet neither Meneptah nor Mesha killed all the Jews or even drove them from their land. They simply won battles against them and described the decisiveness of their victory in terms of absolute destruction. God is using these same idioms to call for Israel to win. He is not asking that every individual die.

- The Amorites were clearly not annihilated. In each of the next two biblical books after Deuteronomy says they were "destroyed," in fact, the Amorite kings are said to still be battling Israel (Josh 10; Judg 11). Even 2 Chronicles, set centuries after Deuteronomy, states that "there were still people left from the . . . Amorites" (2 Chron 8:7).[3]

Despite the appearance of horrific genocide, then, this was no such thing. It was a limited military move to reduce the influence of a genuinely awful movement. God, as he always does, spoke about it in the language of the time. But the Amorites clearly survived for centuries longer.

Note that I wouldn't have "explained away" this awkward part of Scripture. I would simply have suggested we read in it within the context of the wider Old Testament and also of its cultural setting. Then it makes more sense.

Suggested Further Reading

These are a few suggestions of books I have found helpful in my own thinking on topics touched on in *The Myth of the Non-Christian*. Perhaps some will help you. Feel free to contact me directly at luke@chrysolis.org if you want any other recommendations on specific topics.

COMMUNICATING ABOUT JESUS IN A RANGE OF CONTEXTS

Basic Apologetics
Alister McGrath, *Mere Apologetics* (Grand Rapids: Baker, 2012)
John Stackhouse, *Humble Apologetics* (Oxford: Oxford University Press, 2006)

Advanced Apologetics
Clifford Williams, *Existential Reasons for Belief in God: A Defense of Desires and Emotions for Faith* (Downers Grove, IL: InterVarsity Press, 2011)
Benno van den Toren, *Christian Apologetics as Cross-Cultural Dialogue* (New York: Bloomsbury T&T Clark, 2011)

Contextualization
Dean Flemming, *Contextualization in the New Testament* (Downers Grove, IL: InterVarsity Press, 2005)

Philip Jenkins, *The New Faces of Christianity: Believing the Bible in the Global South* (Oxford: Oxford University Press, 2008)

Lamin Sanneh, *Disciples of All Nations* (Oxford: Oxford University Press, 2007)

Evangelism

Rebecca Manley Pippert, *Out of the Saltshaker and into the World* (Downers Grove, IL: InterVarsity Press, 1999)

Rick Richardson, *Reimagining Evangelism* (Downers Grove, IL: InterVarsity Press, 2006)

Conversion

David M. Holley, *Meaning and Mystery: What It Means to Believe in God* (Malden, MA: Wiley-Blackwell, 2010)

Scot McKnight, *Turning to Jesus: The Sociology of Conversion in the New Testament* (Louisville: Westminster John Knox, 2002)

Doug Schaupp and Don Everts, *I Once Was Lost* (Downers Grove, IL: InterVarsity Press, 2008)

Gordon Smith, *Beginning Well* (Downers Grove, IL: InterVarsity Press, 2001)

UNDERSTANDING AND RESPONDING TO DIFFERENT GROUPS

Spiritual But Not Religious People

Linda Mercadante, *Belief Without Borders* (Oxford: Oxford University Press, 2014)

John Drane, *Do Christians Know How to Be Spiritual?* (London: Darton, Longman and Todd, 2005)

Ellis Potter, *Three Theories of Everything* (Switzerland: Destinée, 2012)

Atheists

Contemporary and Historical Overviews

The Oxford Handbook of Atheism, ed. Stephen Bullivant and Michael Ruse (Oxford: Oxford University Press, 2013)

Alister McGrath, *The Twilight of Atheism* (London: Rider, 2005)

New Atheist Texts

Richard Dawkins, *The God Delusion* (London: Random House, 2006)

Christopher Hitchens, *God Is Not Great* (New York: Atlantic Books, 2007)

Christian Responses to New Atheism

John Lennox, *Gunning for God: Why the New Atheists Are Missing the Target* (London: Lion, 2011)

Alister McGrath, *The Dawkins Delusion* (Downers Grove, IL: InterVarsity Press, 2010)

Francis Spufford, *Unapologetic* (New York: HarperCollins, 2013)

Nominal Christians

David Kinnaman, with Aly Hawkins, *You Lost Me: Why Young Christians Are Leaving Church . . . and Rethinking Faith* (Grand Rapids: Baker Books, 2011)

Scot McKnight and Hauna Ondrey, *Finding Faith, Losing Faith: Stories of Conversion and Apostasy* (Waco, TX: Baylor University Press, 2008)

Christian Smith, *Souls in Transition* (Oxford: Oxford University Press, 2009)

SPECIFIC QUESTIONS

Suffering

David Bentley Hart, *The Doors of the Sea: Where Was God in the Tsunami?* (Grand Rapids: Eerdmans, 2011)

John Stackhouse, *Can God Be Trusted?* (Downers Grove, IL: InterVarsity Press, 2008)

God of the Old Testament

Paul Copan, *Is God a Moral Monster? Making Sense of the Old Testament God* (Grand Rapids: Baker, 2011)

Christopher Wright, *Old Testament Ethics for the People of God* (Downers Grove, IL: InterVarsity Press, 2004)

Historical and Contemporary Failures of Christians

William T. Cavanaugh, *The Myth of Religious Violence* (Oxford: Oxford University Press, 2009)

David Bentley Hart, *Atheist Delusions: The Christian Revolution and Its Fashionable Enemies* (New Haven, CT: Yale University Press, 2009)
Dan Kimball, *Adventures in Churchland* (Grand Rapids: Zondervan, 2011)
Rodney Stark, *The Triumph of Christianity: How the Jesus Movement Became the World's Largest Religion* (New York: HarperOne, 2011)

Christian Spirituality
Alister McGrath, *Christian Spirituality* (Malden, MA: Wiley-Blackwell, 1999)
Eugene Peterson, *Christ Plays in Ten Thousand Places* (Grand Rapids: Eerdmans, 2008)
Rick Richardson, *Experiencing Healing Prayer* (Downers Grove, IL: Inter-Varsity Press, 2005)

Reimagining Church
Neil Cole, *Church 3.0* (San Francisco: Jossey-Bass, 2010)
Alan Hirsch, *The Forgotten Ways* (Grand Rapids: Brazos, 2006)
Rick Richardson, *Evangelism Outside the Box* (Downers Grove, IL: Inter-Varsity Press, 2000)

God and Science

Basic
John Lennox, *God's Undertaker* (Oxford: Lion, 2011)
Jonathan Sacks, *The Great Partnership: Science, Religion and the Search for Meaning* (New York: Schocken Books, 2011)

Advanced
David Bentley Hart, *The Experience of God* (New Haven, CT: Yale University Press, 2013)
Alvin Plantinga, *Where the Conflict Really Lies: Science, Religion and Naturalism* (Oxford: Oxford University Press, 2011)

Religious Pluralism
Ravi Zacharias, *Jesus Among Other Gods* (Nashville: Thomas Nelson, 2000)

Miracles
Craig Keener, *Miracles: The Credibility of the New Testament Accounts* (Grand Rapids: Baker, 2011)
C. S. Lewis, *Miracles* (New York: HarperOne, 2015)

The Resurrection

Basic

Gary R. Habermas and Michael R. Licona, *The Case for the Resurrection of Jesus* (Grand Rapids: Kregel, 2004)

Advanced

N. T. Wright, *The Resurrection of the Son of God* (Minneapolis: Fortress, 2003)

Christianity as Wish Fulfillment

Amy Orr-Ewing, *Is Believing in God Irrational?* (Downers Grove, IL: InterVarsity Press, 2008)

Being Good and Happy Without God

Dietrich Bonhoeffer, *The Cost of Discipleship* (New York: Touchstone, 1995)

Kenda Creasy Dean, *Almost Christian* (Oxford: Oxford University Press, 2011)

Salvation by Works

Philip Yancey, *What's So Amazing About Grace?* (Grand Rapids: Zondervan, 2002)

Acknowledgments

My first thanks go to you—friendly reader—for buying, borrowing or simply casually perusing this book. I appreciate your time spent here, and I hope it has proved useful and enjoyable for you!

What you have read has been particularly shaped by several people, and I want to give them each a nod of thanks:

First, my parents. I've always said that when I write a book I would mention their huge influence. Both of them instilled in me a passion for reading, and some of my earliest memories are of sitting on the floor sounding out words from a picture book with my mother. My dad is the person who most enabled me to become a writer. Between the ages of sixteen and eighteen I had to produce four original essays a week in school. Dad read every single one of them. He gave me detailed feedback to help me make my style clearer and easier to read. He said to me repeatedly that "you can have the best ideas in the world but if you can't write well, then you won't be able to share them with anyone." So he deserves credit if you understood or enjoyed anything I wrote in this book.

Second, my wife, Whitney, has been involved in every stage of this book. We had a baby and moved houses several thousand miles during the time I was writing. She has been amazing at permitting me space to write even within all this upheaval. Whitney is also the best critical reader I know, and her feedback and input have been invaluable. She is also just an all-round beautiful person, who is funny and clever and loves Jesus a lot, and for whom I am beyond thankful! Our children— Jackson, Will and Amélie—are as blessed to have her as their mother as I am to be her husband.

Third, Rick Richardson has been a big influence. We got to know each other several years ago when I was studying under him for my master's degree at Wheaton College. Rick has been a mentor, friend and encourager. He was the first person to seriously suggest to me that I should write a book. When we hung out together at the 2012 Olympics he spent the entire two-hour car journey asking me questions like, "When are you going to write?" "If you had to write a book what would it be about?" and "Who would be your audience?" It was a year later when we were working together on a project at the Burning Man festival that the idea for this book first came to me. I talked it through with Rick, and he said with great conviction, "This book needs to be written, and you are the one who needs to write it." A few months later he took the time to read my first draft chapters/outline and give me detailed feedback. So Rick Richardson has his fingerprints all over this book.

Fourth, my friend Jessica Leep Fick was kind enough to spend time emailing and skyping me early in the writing process. She had just had the proposal for her excellent IVP book *Beautiful Feet* accepted, and without her insights into the submission process I would have had a much longer and harder road to publication.

Other friends who helpfully read and gave feedback on draft chapters and sections include Phil Andrews, Lucian Balanescu, Hannah Giddings, Nik and Claire Hookey, Krisztina Mair, Caitlin Ormiston, Simon Richiardi and Lauren Sugden (now Lauren Brabbs).

My current wider ministry, and freedom to also write, has been made possible by the many friends who support Chrysolis financially and in prayer. I am blessed to be part of a big team in this way, and it's been so encouraging that people want to be involved in our work. Thank you!

I would especially like to thank Chrysolis's board of trustees—Nik, Krisztina, Caitlin, Lauren, Hannah and Trevor Raaff—along with past members Benedict Cambridge and Ashley Cooper. Krisztina sometimes says that the dream in life is "doing ministry with your mates," and I think she's onto something there.

Many people were kind enough to be interviewed by me and to subsequently proofread my accounts of our conversations. Their willingness to gift me their ideas and experience has made this a much better book than it would have been if it were based only on my own thoughts and reading. So, my appreciation here goes to Kate, Lucian, Freda, Ann Cawley, Gordon Crowther, Joey Espinosa, Mihaela Gingirov, Andrew Givens, David Godfrey, Nate Gordon, Michael Green, Stefan Gustavsson, Greg Johnson, Dan Kimball, Karen Lawrence, Krisztina, York Moore, Emi Ologeanu, Rick, Tamara Sanchez-Kapostasy, Nasrin Sjogren, Martin Smith, Nicole Voelkel and Mike York. One or two of your interviews weren't directly cited, but your influence is still felt.

I hugely appreciate that IVP, and most especially my editor, Al Hsu, have taken on and believed in this project. They have been great guides during its development. I love IVP, and their books have been a tremendous influence in my own development. It is a privilege to now also be an IVP author.

Finally, I am thankful to our Father God for his faithfulness and patience with me, and for letting me be part of his work in the world in ways that constantly surprise me. Slavă Domnului!

Notes

ONE: FLEXIBILITY

[1]Tabatha Leggett, "Inside Alpha: An Atheist's Foray into Christianity," *New Statesman* (June 2013), www.newstatesman.com/religion/2013/06/inside-alpha-atheists-foray-christianity.

[2]Alister McGrath, *Mere Apologetics* (Grand Rapids: Baker, 2012), 15.

[3]John Stackhouse, *Humble Apologetics* (Oxford: Oxford University Press, 2006), 115.

[4]Klyne Snodgrass, *Stories with Intent* (Grand Rapids: Eerdmans, 2008), 37.

[5]Unless otherwise indicated, the statistics in this section are drawn from page 4 of Pew Research Center, "America's Changing Religious Landscape," May 12, 2015, www.pewforum.org/files/2015/05/RLS-05-08-full-report.pdf.

[6]Gallup, "In U.S., Four in 10 Report Attending Church in Last Week" December 24, 2013, www.gallup.com/poll/166613/four-report-attending-church-last-week.aspx.

[7]Pew Research Center, "'Nones' on the Rise: One-in-Five Adults Have No Religious Affiliation," October 9, 2012, www.pewforum.org/2012/10/09/nones-on-the-rise/.

TWO: PLAUSIBILITY AND DESIRABILITY

[1]Jürgen Moltmann, "2007 Moltmann Moments: Hope (Part 1 of 3)," Day of Common Learning Lecture, Seattle Pacific University, September 20, 2007, paper 62, http://digitalcommons.spu.edu/av_events/62.

[2]Nicholas Wolterstorff, *Lament for a Son* (Grand Rapids: Eerdmans, 1997), 91.

[3]I owe this insight to John Lennox, whom I have heard make this point repeatedly in lectures and talks.

[4]John Lennox, *God's Undertaker* (Oxford: Lion, 2011), 16.

[5]Ibid.

[6]C. S. Lewis, *Screwtape Proposes a Toast, and Other Pieces* (London: Fontana, 1970), 58.

[7]Michael Buckley, *Denying and Disclosing God: The Ambiguous Progress of Modern Atheism* (New Haven, CT: Yale University Press, 2004), 138.

THREE: TANGIBILITY

[1]Switchfoot, "Dare You to Move," released January 1, 2000, on *The Beautiful Letdown*, Columbia/Red Ink, Compact Disc.

[2]Gustav Mahler, *Gustav Mahler Symphonies Nos. 1 and 2 in Full Score* (Mineola, NY: Dover Publications, 1987), 378.

[3]Doug Yeo, "The Puzzle of Our Lives," blog entry, www.yeodoug.com/articles/puzzle/puzzle.html.

[4]Terms borrowed from the excellent Doug Schaupp and Don Everts, *I Once Was Lost* (Downers Grove, IL: InterVarsity Press, 2008).

[5]Blaise Pascal, *Pensées* (London: Penguin, 1995), 4.

[6]My thanks here go especially to James Choung, national director of evangelism for InterVarsity Christian Fellowship, who suggested the term *tangibility* as an ideal fit for what I was trying to say.

[7]Alan Hirsch, *The Forgotten Ways* (Grand Rapids: Brazos, 2006), 41.

[8]This description of Ephesus is drawn both from inferences within the text of Acts and also I. Howard Marshall, A. R. Millard, J. I. Packer and Donald Wiseman, eds., *New Bible Dictionary*, 3rd ed. (Downers Grove, IL: InterVarsity Press, 1996), 328-29.

[9]Ben Witherington III, *The Acts of the Apostles* (Grand Rapids: Eerdmans, 1998), 574.

[10]Acts 19:19 says the "the value of the scrolls . . . came to fifty thousand drachmas." Ben Witherington says that a drachma was a day's wages (Ibid., 582). Assuming that a person worked six days a week without vacation (312 days a year), it would take more than 160 years for them to work 50,000 days.

[11]C. S Lewis, *Miracles* (Glasgow: Fount, 1984), 98.

[12]Ibid.

FOUR: THE TEMPLE IN THE DESERT AND THE MYSTERIOUS MASSAGE

[1]Ross Thompson and Gareth Williams, *Christian Spirituality* (London: SCM Press, 2008), x.

[2]"The Default State of Atheism," *GBG Atheist News* (blog), November 10, 2007, http://godbegone.blogspot.co.uk/2007/11/default-state-of-atheism.html.

[3]Justin L. Barrett, "Cognitive Science of Religion: What Is It and Why Is It?" *Religion Compass* 1, no. 6 (2007): 755.

[4]Ibid., 754.

[5]Justin L. Barrett, *Born Believers: The Science of Children's Religious Belief* (New York: Free Press, 2012), 3.

[6]WIN-Gallup International, 2012. "Global Index of Religion and Atheism," July 27, 2012, www.wingia.com/web/files/news/14/file/14.pdf.

[7]Terry Pratchett, *Feet of Clay* (London: Corgi, 1997), 96.

[8]James Sire does a great job of describing the "New Age" in James Sire, *The Universe Next Door* (Downers Grove, IL: InterVarsity Press, 2004), 162-210.

[9]A minority of people even use the label and also happily maintain some level of continuing church attendance or involvement. Some such individuals are interviewed in Linda Mercadante, *Belief Without Borders* (Oxford: Oxford University Press, 2014).

[10]"Interview with Ray Caesar," *This Is So Contemporary* (blog), June 8, 2012, http://thisissocontemporary.com/?interview=ray-caesar (accessed June 11, 2013).

FIVE: DOES CHRISTIANITY ENABLE A RICHER SPIRITUALITY?

[1]Ursula Le Guin, *A Wizard of Earthsea* (London: Puffin, 1971), 53.

[2]Ibid., 52.

[3]Mercadante uses the terms *horizontal* and *vertical* instead of *outwards* and *upwards*. Linda Mercadante, *Belief Without Borders* (Oxford: Oxford University Press, 2014)

[4]Some people with a primarily outwards spirituality might also be atheists. They will likely have a blend of the questions in this chapter and the more plausibility-focused ones discussed in chapter eight.

[5]See, for example, the writings of Alan Hirsch, Michael Frost, Neil Cole and Dan Kimball, and InterVarsity Press's Forge line of books.

[6]Aleksandr Solzhenitsyn, *The Gulag Archipelago* (London: Harvill, 2003), 75.

[7]Paul Allen Pruett, "Psychology of Religion: What Do People Mean When They Say 'I Am Not Religious, but I Am Spiritual?'" *Quora* (April 23, 2014), www.quora.com/Psychology-of-Religion/What-do-people-mean -when-they-say-I-am-not-religious-but-I-am-spiritual.

[8]Rich Mullins, "All the Way to Kingdom Come," from *The Jesus Record*, Myrhh, 1998.

[9]R. K. McGregor Wright, "God, Metaphor and Gender," in *Discovering Biblical Equality*, ed. Ronald W. Pierce and Rebecca Merrill Groothuis (Downers Grove, IL: InterVarsity Press, 2005), 298.

[10]Ibid., 297.

[11]Jesus certainly is a man. But as Paul writes to the Galatians, "God sent his Son, born of a woman … to redeem" humanity (Gal 4:4-5). Salvation comes when a genderless person of the godhead becomes fully male. But that male enters the world via a female. Thus, as Thomas Oden phrases it, "Both genders were honored equally in the incarnation." Thomas Oden, *Classic Christianity* (New York: HarperOne, 1992), 265.

SIX: INVITING OTHERS INTO AN EXPERIENCE OF
CHRISTIAN SPIRITUALITY

[1]"Motorcycle Drive-by," by Third Eye Blind, *Third Eye Blind*, Elektra, 1997.

[2]Armand Barus, "Spirituality," in *Dictionary of Mission Theology*, ed. John Corrie (Downers Grove, IL: InterVarsity Press, 2007), 372.

[3]Simon Chan, "Spirituality," in *Global Dictionary of Theology*, ed. William A. Dyrness and Veli-Matti Kärkkäinen (Downers Grove, IL: InterVarsity Press, 2008), 852.

[4]John Goldingay, *Old Testament Theology, Vol. 1, Israel's Gospel* (Downers Grove, IL: InterVarsity Press, 2003), 20.

SEVEN: DAWKINS ON A BIKE

[1]Gus Holwerda, *The Unbelievers*, directed by Gus Holwerda Black Chalk Productions, 2013.

[2]Other leading New Atheists include philosopher-neurologist Sam Harris, philosopher Daniel Dennett, physicist-philosopher Victor Stenger, former Pentecostal preacher Dan Barker, philosopher AC Grayling and the late journalist Christopher Hitchens.

[3]Julian Baggini, *Atheism: A Very Short Introduction* (Oxford: Oxford University Press, 2003), 3.

[4]The terms used by philosopher-theologian Keith Ward to summarize the charges leveled by New Atheists against religion.

[5]Alain de Botton, *Religion for Atheists* (London: Penguin, 2012), 19.

[6]Statistics drawn (with my rephrasing) from Ryan T. Cragun, Joseph H. Hammer and Jesse M. Smith, "North America," in *The Oxford Handbook of Atheism*, ed. Stephen Bullivant and Michael Ruse (Oxford: Oxford University Press, 2013), 604-8.

[7]Ibid., 603.

[8]The two other major differences are that US atheists are 66% male, and also overwhelmingly more likely to live in urban centers of more than 100,000 people. The concentration in more populous areas is probably down to new/emerging ideas typically being more readily adopted in cities. The appeal of atheism to men, along with its correlating lack of attraction for women, has less readily obvious causes, though I'm sure some possible reasons will spring to your mind. See Cragun, Hammer and Smith, "North America."

[9]J. J. Exline, C. L. Park, J. M. Smyth and M. P. Carey, "Anger Toward God: Social-Cognitive Predictors, Prevalence, and Links with Adjustment to Bereavement and Cancer," *Journal of Personality and Social Psychology* 100, no. 1 (2011): 129-48.

[10]Julie Juola Exline and Alyce Martin, "Anger Towards God: A New Frontier in Forgiveness Research," in *Handbook of Forgiveness*, ed. Everett L. Worthington Jr. (New York: Routledge, 2005), 73-88.

[11]M. Rodriguez, "I Don't Believe in God, but I Still Hate Him Anyways," *The BitterSweet End* (blog), February 9, 2014, http://bittersweetend.wordpress .com/2014/02/09/i-dont-believe-in-god-but-i-still-hate-him-anyways/.

[12]Brian Mountford, *Christian Atheist* (Winchester: O Books, 2011), 13-14.

[13]Ibid., 14.

[14]Conducted by TNS Opinion & Social on request of European Commission, Biotechnology, 2010, 204.

[15]Brendan O'Neill, "How Atheists Became the Most Colossally Smug and Annoying People on the Planet," *The Telegraph*, August 14, 2013, http:// blogs.telegraph.co.uk/news/brendanoneill2/100230985/how-atheists-became-the-most-colossally-smug-and-annoying-people-on-the-planet/.

[16]G. K. Chesterton, *Orthodoxy* (London: Fontana, 1961), 137.

[17]For an alternate take on this cry of Jesus, see Al Hsu, "He's Calling for

Elijah! Why We Still Mishear Jesus," *Christianity Today* (April 2012), www
.christianitytoday.com/ct/2012/aprilweb-only/my-god-forsaken-me.html.

[18]Tomáš Halík, *Patience with God: The Story of Zacchaeus Continuing in Us*
(New York: Doubleday Religious, 2009). Kindle ed., loc. 29-33.

[19]Ibid., 607.

[20]"Atheism, Class and Education," *Theos*, October 5, 2009, www.theos
thinktank.co.uk/comment/2009/10/05/atheism-class-and-education.

[21]For example, visit www.patheos.com/Atheist.

EIGHT: ISN'T FAITH IN GOD IRRATIONAL AND OUTDATED?

[1]Ricky Gervais, interview by Piers Morgan, "Piers Morgan Tonight," CNN,
February 16, 2012.

[2]Richard Dawkins, *The God Delusion* (London: Random House, 2006), 77.

[3]Victor Stenger, "Atheism and the Physical Sciences," in *The Oxford Handbook
of Atheism*, ed. Stephen Bullivant and Michael Ruse (Oxford: Oxford University Press, 2013), 446.

[4]Mary Midgley, *Science and Poetry* (New York: Routledge, 2006), 112-14.

[5]Ibid., 71.

[6]John Polkinghorne, *Quarks, Chaos and Christianity: Questions to Science and
Religion* (London: SPCK, 1997), 15.

[7]Ibid.

[8]C. S. Lewis, *The Voyage of the Dawn Treader* (London: Fontana, 1984), 158-59.

[9]David Bentley Hart, *Atheist Delusions* (New Haven, CT: Yale University
Press, 2009), 71.

[10]Quotation and list of names, along with my choice of quotes from Lewis
and Bacon in this section, taken from John Lennox, *God's Undertaker*
(London: Lion, 2011), 21.

[11]Ibid.

[12]C. S. Lewis, *Miracles* (Glasgow: Fontana, 1984), 110.

[13]Vishal Mangalwadi, *The Book That Made Your World: How the Bible Created
the Soul of Western Civilization* (Nashville: Thomas Nelson, 2011), 244-45.

[14]John Lennox, *Gunning for God* (London: Lion, 2011), 48.

[15]I owe the basic argument of this section to the one advanced in David Bentley
Hart, *The Experience of God* (New Haven, CT: Yale University Press, 2013).

[16]Helen Lewis, "If We Could Prove String Theory Wrong, I Would Be
Thrilled!," *New Statesman* (June 11, 2011), www.newstatesman.com/blogs/
helen-lewis-hasteley/2011/06/physics-theory-ideas-universe.

[17]Ricky Gervais, "Does God Exist? Ricky Gervais Takes Your Questions," *The Wall Street Journal* (December 22, 2010), http://blogs.wsj.com/speakeasy/2010/12/22/does-god-exist-ricky-gervais-takes-your-questions/.

[18]Most sources will give you similar figures, but one very easily accessible summary is found in the statistical tables of: Pew Research Center, "The Global Religious Landscape" (2012).

[19]It does often surprise people, especially those who assume that all religions are the same, that most forms of Buddhism are—in fact—atheistic. Widely respected Buddhist monk and scholar Nyanaponika Thera, for example, writes that "the idea of a personal deity, a creator god conceived to be eternal and omnipotent, is incompatible with the Buddha's teachings." *Buddhism and the God-Idea*, ed. Nyanaponika Thera (Kandy, Sri Lanka: Buddhist Publication Society, 2008).

[20]Significant strands within each of these two religions affirm the existence a single divine, even personal, power that is ultimately the source of all reality. In Vedanta Hinduism, for example, this is called the Brahman. But none of these religions consistently spotlight any particular claim that the divine has chosen to "manifest itself, or appear, even less enter into the world." Keith Ward, *Images of Eternity* (Oxford: Oneworld, 1993), 21.

[21]This command to read the Injil is recognized by most Muslims, though they tend to insist that the contents of the Gospels became corrupted over the centuries between Jesus' death and Muhammad's birth. Some of this chapter addresses that charge, but because this section is on engaging atheists, I refer readers interested in engaging with Muslims to Nabeel Qureshi, *Seeking Allah, Finding Jesus* (Grand Rapids: Zondervan, 2014); Richard Shumack, *The Wisdom of Islam and the Foolishness of Christianity* (Sydney: Island View, 2014); Chawkat Moucarry, *Faith to Faith* (Leicester, UK: Inter-Varsity Press, 2001).

[22]D. A. Carson and Douglas Moo, *An Introduction to the New Testament* (Leicester, UK: Apollos, 2005), 182.

[23]Ibid., 152, 207.

[24]William Lane Craig, *Reasonable Faith* (Wheaton, IL: Crossway, 2008), 334.

[25]Lucian's diagrams and my argument in this section draw on F. F. Bruce, *The New Testament Documents: Are They Reliable?* (Downers Grove, IL: Inter-Varsity Press, 1981); William Lane Craig, "Can We Trust the Bible Written 2000 Years Ago?" YouTube video, 2:24, posted by "100 Huntley," June 1, 2009, www.youtube.com/watch?v=reYBCz_kf1c.

[26]The beginning of the list is missing, so the Gospels of Matthew and Mark are actually omitted from what we have left of the Muratorian Fragment, though it is widely agreed that they were on the original list.

[27]A helpful online resource that compiles writings, orthodox and heretical, from the early centuries after Jesus is *Early Christian Writings*. It includes a handy tool where you can search through all the Scripture quotations used by early Christian writers: www.earlychristianwritings.com/e-catena/.

[28]H. B. Swete, *The Gospel of St. Peter: The Text in English and Greek, with Introduction, Notes and Indices* (Eugene, OR: Wipf & Stock, 2005), 27.

[29]Matthew Parris, "If Jesus Did Not Exist, the Church Would Not Invent Him," *The Spectator* (April 22, 2006), www.spectator.co.uk/columnists/matthew-parris/15182/if-jesus-did-not-exist-the-church-would-not-invent-him/.

[30]Craig Keener, *Miracles* (Grand Rapids: Baker Academic, 2011), 21-106.

[31]Ibid., 68.

[32]Ibid., 21.

[33]C. S. Lewis, *Mere Christianity* (Glasgow: Collins, 1977), 118-19.

[34]This argument is often referred to as "the argument from desire" and Peter Kreeft offers a good summary here: Peter Kreeft and Ronald K. Tacelli, *Handbook of Christian Apologetics* (Downers Grove, IL: InterVarsity Press, 1994), 78-81.

[35]Rosanna Greenstreet, "Q&A: Phil Daniels," *The Guardian*, July 12, 2014, www.theguardian.com/lifeandstyle/2014/jul/12/phil-daniels-interview.

[36]Frederick Buechner, *Wishful Thinking* (London: Mowbray, 1993), 5.

[37]Thomas Nagel, *The Last Word* (Oxford: Oxford University Press, 1997), 130.

NINE: CREATING SAFE SPACES FOR EXPLORING QUESTIONS

[1]Doug Schaupp and Don Everts, *I Once Was Lost* (Downers Grove, IL: InterVarsity Press, 2008).

TEN: THE PIMP, THE PLANTER AND THEIR FRIENDS

[1]Doug Schaupp and Don Everts, *I Once Was Lost* (Downers Grove, IL: InterVarsity Press, 2008), 15.

[2]Ibid.

[3]Amnesty International is a great organization, lest I be misunderstood.

[4]David Kinnaman with Aly Hawkins, *You Lost Me: Why Young Christians Are Leaving Church . . . and Rethinking Faith* (Grand Rapids: Baker Books, 2011), 22.

[5]Ibid.

[6]Ibid.

[7]Scot McKnight and Hauna Ondrey, *Finding Faith, Losing Faith: Stories of Conversion and Apostasy* (Waco, TX: Baylor University Press, 2008), 48.

[8]Vern Bengtson with Norella M. Putney and Susan Harris, *Families and Faith: How Religion Is Passed Down Across Generations* (Oxford: Oxford University Press, 2013), 186.

[9]Ibid., 78, 114-15, 117.

[10]J. R. R. Tolkien, *The Lord of the Rings* (London: Unwin, 1978), 186.

[11]Even Saul's famous experience on the road to Damascus, while clearly important in his conversion, wasn't the whole story (Acts 9:1-9). He also needed to subsequently encounter Ananias before he could receive the Holy Spirit, be baptized or encounter Christian community (Acts 9:10-19).

[12]John Stackhouse, *Humble Apologetics* (Oxford: Oxford University Press, 2002), 76.

[13]Gordon Smith, *Beginning Well* (Downers Grove, IL: InterVarsity Press, 2001), 21.

[14]Ibid., 138.

[15]Ibid., 138-56.

[16]Ibid., 139.

[17]Ibid., 180.

ELEVEN: DON'T YOU REALIZE I'VE BEEN THERE AND DONE THAT?

[1]Christian Smith, *Souls in Transition* (Oxford: Oxford University Press, 2009), 154.

[2]John Stott, *The Cross of Christ* (Downers Grove, IL: InterVarsity Press, 1986), 220.

[3]Scot McKnight and Hauna Ondrey, *Finding Faith, Losing Faith: Stories of Conversion and Apostasy* (Waco, TX: Baylor University Press, 2008), 16-42.

[4]C. S. Lewis, *The Problem of Pain* (London: Whitefriars, 1944), 115.

[5]For some more helpful alternative imagery of hell, trying reading C. S. Lewis, *The Great Divorce* (London: HarperCollins, 2000).

[6]Jerry L. Walls, *Hell: The Logic of Damnation* (Notre Dame, IN: University of Notre Dame Press, 1992), 136.

[7]Ibid.

[8]David Kinnaman with Aly Hawkins, *You Lost Me: Why Young Christians Are Leaving Church . . . and Rethinking Faith* (Grand Rapids: Baker Books, 2011), 92.

[9]Read her story in Renée Altson, *Stumbling Toward Faith* (Grand Rapids: Zondervan, 2004).

TWELVE: COMMUNITIES THAT FACILITATE REDISCOVERING JESUS

[1]Marjorie Sykes, *Quakers in India: A Forgotten Century* (London: George Allen & Unwin, 1980), 135.

[2]Rebecca Manley Pippert, *Uncovering the Life of Jesus* (Surrey, UK: The Good Book Company, 2015).

[3]I have heard Michael Green say on many occasions that he finds that posing this question can really help clarify what is holding a person back from following Jesus.

[4]Stefan Paas, "Mission Among Individual Consumers," in *Church After Christendom: New Voices, New Cultures, New Expressions*, ed. Ryan Bolger (Grand Rapids: Baker Academic, 2012), 153.

[5]Ibid., 160.

[6]Further details to York's approach appear in York Moore, *Growing Your Faith by Giving It Away* (Downers Grove, IL: InterVarsity Press, 2005), and York Moore, *Making All Things New* (Downers Grove, IL: InterVarsity Press, 2012).

EPILOGUE

[1]Rick Richardson, *Reimagining Evangelism* (Downers Grove, IL: InterVarsity Press, 2006), 43.

APPENDIX 1: COMPARATIVE STATISTICS

[1]The statistics in this section are drawn from Statistics Canada, the Canadian federal government agency that compiles and analyzes national statistics. Statistics Canada, National Household Survey (NHS) Profile, "2011 National Household Survey," *Ottawa: Statistics Canada Catalogue no. 99-004-XWE* (September 11, 2013), www12.statcan.gc.ca/nhs-enm/2011/dp-pd/prof/index.cfm?Lang=E; and Colin Lindsay, "Canadians Attend Weekly Religious Services Less Than 20 Years Ago," *Statistics Canada* (modified November 11th, 2008), www.statcan.gc.ca/pub/89-630-x/2008001/article/10650-eng.htm/.

[2]Richard Johnson, "Religion in Canada: Mostly for Mum & Dad," *National Post*, December 21, 2012, news.nationalpost.com/news/graphics/polling-religion-in-canada.

[3]Ryan T. Cragun, Joseph H. Hammer and Jesse M. Smith, "North America," in *The Oxford Handbook of Atheism*, ed. Stephen Bullivant and Michael Ruse (Oxford: Oxford University Press, 2013), 603.

[4]Office for National Statistics, *Religion in England and Wales 2011*, December 11, 2012, www.ons.gov.uk/ons/rel/census/2011-census/key-statistics-for -local-authorities-in-england-and-wales/rpt-religion.html. "'One in 10' Attends Church Weekly," *BBC News*, April 3, 2007, http://news.bbc.co.uk/1 /hi/uk/6520463.stm.

[5]"40% of Adults Pray, Says Survey," *BBC News*, November 11, 2007, http:// news.bbc.co.uk/1/hi/uk/7089139.stm; "Spiritual but Not Religious," *BBC News*, January 3, 2013, www.bbc.co.uk/news/magazine-20888141.

[6]William Jordan, "A Third of British Adults Don't Believe in a Higher Power," *YouGov*, February 12, 2015, https://yougov.co.uk/news/2015/02/12/ third-british-adults-dont-believe-higher-power/.

APPENDIX 2: DID GOD COMMAND GENOCIDE?

[1]Paul Copan, *Is God a Moral Monster? Making Sense of the Old Testament God* (Grand Rapids: Baker, 2011), 172.

[2]Ibid.

[3]All the bullet-pointed arguments here about the Amorite genocides are largely drawn or adapted from the work of apologist Paul Copan, and there is very little here original to me. See Copan, *Is God A Moral Monster?* and *When God Goes to Starbucks* (Grand Rapids: Baker, 2008).

About the Author

Luke Cawley is the director of Chrysolis, an organization that he helped establish. Chrysolis's accent is on catalyzing the journeys of individuals toward God and of Christian communities toward greater missional effectiveness.

Much of Luke's time is spent in contexts where God is not typically discussed in depth. He loves engaging with skeptical audiences in universities, schools, bars, cafés and theaters. He also enjoys enabling individuals and Christian communities to better engage those around them with the story of Jesus.

Luke previously spent many years in the United Kingdom and Romania working with the International Fellowship of Evangelical Students movements there. Part of his focus was on planting and developing new missional communities on university campuses that previously lacked any collective Christian witness. He has also worked for a press agency and been a newspaper columnist, and was part of the writing team for InterVarsity Christian Fellowship's evangelism department.

He has an MA in evangelism and leadership from Wheaton College in Illinois, and a CTPS in Christian apologetics from Oxford University. While at Wheaton he was elected by the faculty of the Billy Graham Center for Evangelism to receive the Robert E. Coleman Award for Evangelism and Leadership. During his time in Oxford he also graduated from the Oxford Centre for Christian Apologetics. Luke also holds a BA (with honors) in English Literature from Cardiff University, where much of his studies focused on children's literature and crime fiction.

Luke is married to a South Carolinian elementary school teacher, Whitney, and they have three young children: Jackson, Will and Amélie. Toward the end of writing this book their family relocated to Bucharest, Romania, to spend a few years developing the work of Chrysolis in Eastern Europe. Luke continues, though, to make regular ministry visits to the US and his homeland of the United Kingdom.

You can read Luke's writing online at LukeCawley.org and Chrysolis.org, follow his tweets at @chrysolis and @lukecawley, or drop him an email at luke@chrysolis.org.